Cambridge Elements ≡

Elements in the Gothic
edited by
Dale Townshend
Manchester Metropolitan University
Angela Wright
University of Sheffield

FOLK GOTHIC

Dawn Keetley
Lehigh University

CAMBRIDGE
UNIVERSITY PRESS

Shaftesbury Road, Cambridge CB2 8EA, United Kingdom

One Liberty Plaza, 20th Floor, New York, NY 10006, USA

477 Williamstown Road, Port Melbourne, VIC 3207, Australia

314–321, 3rd Floor, Plot 3, Splendor Forum, Jasola District Centre, New Delhi – 110025, India

103 Penang Road, #05–06/07, Visioncrest Commercial, Singapore 238467

Cambridge University Press is part of Cambridge University Press & Assessment, a department of the University of Cambridge.

We share the University's mission to contribute to society through the pursuit of education, learning and research at the highest international levels of excellence.

www.cambridge.org
Information on this title: www.cambridge.org/9781009467810

DOI: 10.1017/9781009160902

First published 2023

A catalogue record for this publication is available from the British Library

ISBN 978-1-009-46781-0 Hardback
ISBN 978-1-009-16089-6 Paperback
ISSN 2634-8721 (online)
ISSN 2634-8713 (print)

Folk Gothic

Elements in the Gothic

DOI: 10.1017/9781009160902
First published online: December 2023

Dawn Keetley
Lehigh University
Author for correspondence: Dawn Keetley, dek7@lehigh.edu

Abstract: *Folk Gothic* begins with the assertion that a significant part of what has been categorised as folk horror is more accurately and usefully labelled as Folk Gothic. Through the modifier 'folk', Folk Gothic obviously shares with folk horror its deployment (and frequent fabrication) of diegetic folklore. Folk Gothic does not share, however, folk horror's incarnate monsters, its forward impetus across spatial and ontological boundaries and the shock and repulsion elicited through its bodily violence. The author argues that the Folk Gothic as a literary, televisual and cinematic formation is defined by particular temporal and spatial structures that serve to forge distinctly non-human stories. In emphasising these temporal and spatial structures – not literal 'folk' and 'monsters' – the Folk Gothic tells stories that foreground land and 'things', consequently loosening the grip of anthropocentrism.

This Element also has a video abstract: www.cambridge.org/folk-gothic

Keywords: Gothic, folk horror, British literature, film and television, horror

ISBNs: 9781009467810 (HB), 9781009160896 (PB), 9781009160902 (OC)
ISSNs: 2634-8721 (online), 2634-8713 (print)

Contents

1 Folk Gothic

Since around 2010, folk horror has emerged as an important object of both academic and popular critical study. This Element begins with the claim that 'folk horror' as a category has been defined too diffusely, its boundaries stretched too far. As Keith McDonald and Wayne Johnson aptly put it, folk horror is often a 'flimsy and unsatisfactory moniker' for a 'broad range of cultural artefacts'.[1] More particularly, I argue that a large part of what has been categorised as folk horror is more accurately and usefully labelled as Folk Gothic.[2] This section will address what Folk Gothic shares with folk horror and what makes it substantively different.

Although it has roots in the late nineteenth- and early twentieth-century fiction of Thomas Hardy, M. R. James, Arthur Machen and Algernon Blackwood, folk horror emerged as a distinct category with three British films of the late 1960s and early 1970s: *Witchfinder General* (Michael Reeves, 1968), *The Blood on Satan's Claw* (Piers Haggard, 1971) and *The Wicker Man* (Robin Hardy, 1973). Since about 2010, folk horror has been experiencing a second wave characterised by both a heightened interest in 'first-wave' folk horror of the 1960s and 1970s and an almost dizzying proliferation of new cultural productions – a proliferation that is due in part at least to the tendency to label anything 'folk horror' if it seems even partly to fall in that (loose) category.[3] As Steve Neale has noted, a 'genre's history is as much the history of a term as it is of the films to which the term has been applied'. The '*institutionalization* of any generic term', he continues, 'is a key aspect of the social existence – and hence the potential social significance – of any genre'.[4] Although the term folk horror has a relatively long history, it did not

---

[1] Keith McDonald, and Wayne Johnson, *Contemporary Gothic and Horror Film* (London: Anthem Press, 2021), p. 57.

[2] See Dawn Keetley, '*True Detective*'s Folk Gothic', in Justin Edwards, Rune Graulund and Johan Höglund (eds.), *Dark Scenes from Damaged Earth: The Gothic Anthropocene* (Minneapolis, MN: University of Minnesota Press, 2022), pp. 130–50.

[3] For critical discussions of folk horror, see especially Paul Newland, 'Folk Horror and the Contemporary Cult of British Rural Landscape: The Case of *Blood on Satan's Claw*', in Paul Newland (ed.), *British Landscapes on Film* (Manchester: Manchester University Press, 2016), pp. 162–79; Adam Scovell, *Folk Horror: Hours Dreadful and Things Strange* (Leighton Buzzard: Auteur, 2017); Paul Cowdell, '"Practising Witchcraft Myself during the Filming": Folk Horror, Folklore, and the Folkloresque', *Western Folklore*, 78:4 (Fall 2019): 295–326; Dawn Keetley, 'Defining Folk Horror', *Revenant: Critical and Creative Studies of the Supernatural*, 5 (March 2020): 1–32 (and the essays in the special issue for which this essay is an introduction); *Woodlands Dark and Days Bewitched: A History of Folk Horror*, directed by Kier-La Janisse (Severin Films, 2021); Jamie Chambers, 'Troubling Folk Horror: Exoticism, Metonymy, and Solipsism in the 'Unholy Trinity' and Beyond', *JCMS: Journal of Cinema and Media Studies*, 61:2 (Winter 2022): 9–34; Bernice M. Murphy, 'Folk Horror', in Stephen Shapiro and Mark Storey (eds.), *The Cambridge Companion to American Horror* (New York: Cambridge University Press, 2022), pp. 139–53; and Dawn Keetley and Ruth Heholt (eds.), *Folk Horror: New Global Pathways* (Cardiff: University of Wales Press, 2023).

[4] Steve Neale, *Genre and Hollywood* (New York: Routledge, 2000), p. 39; emphasis added.

become a common part of the cultural lexicon – did not become 'institutionalised', to use Neale's term – until after 2010, in the wake of Mark Gatiss's three-part BBC documentary, *A History of Horror*. A landmark in the history of identifying folk horror, Gatiss's *History of Horror* introduces 'folk horror' in part two, 'Home Counties Horrors'. Towards the end of this episode, Gatiss shifts from discussing the dominant Hammer films of the 1960s and articulates a 'new' kind of horror film that avoids what he calls 'the gothic clichés'. 'Amongst these', he claims, 'are a loose collection of films that we might call folk horror'. Gatiss interviews Piers Haggard, director *The Blood on Satan's Claw*, who declares: 'I suppose I was trying to make a folk horror film'.[5] Although this moment was not, in fact, the first use of the term, as is often claimed, it did begin the 'institutionalisation' of folk horror, and that institutionalisation has proceeded apace.[6]

Rick Altman argues in his 'theory of genre analysis' that the task of the critic must diverge from that of those in the film and media industries; although the latter may have constructed a loose genre – what he calls the 'industrial/journalistic term' – the task of the genre critic is to create a more precise definition: '*the constitution of a corpus comprises one of the genre critic's most important tasks*', he writes.[7] The critic does so by identifying and describing 'certain traits and systems present and operative within a large number of the texts constituted by the preliminary corpus'.[8] When subjecting the genres of both 'folk horror' and Folk Gothic to such analysis, the place to begin is with what they share – the modifier 'folk'.

1.1 The 'Folk' of Folk Horror and Folk Gothic

Both folk horror and the Folk Gothic are centrally defined by their uses of both 'folk' and 'folklore'. They do more than merely rely on folklore for certain thematic elements, however. Folk horror and Folk Gothic are specifically defined through their *weaving of folklore as anachronism into and as a critical part of the diegesis*: folk tales – along with the function and meanings of folklore – are overt and thematised aspects of the narrative. There are frequent scenes that involves protagonists poring over old woodcuts and books or conducting internet searches about folk tales that characters come to realise are driving the plots within which they are enmeshed (Figure 1). In Peter A. Dowling's 2016 film *Sacrifice*, for example, based on Sharon Bolton's 2008 novel of the same name, the protagonist, Tora Hamilton (Radha Mitchell),

---

[5] *A History of Horror with Mark Gatiss*, ep. 2, 'Home Counties Horror', John Das (Director), BBC, 18 October 2010.

[6] For the earlier history of 'folk horror' as a generic term, see Keetley, 'Defining', p. 1, fn.2.

[7] Rick Altman, *The American Musical Film* (Bloomington, IN: Indiana University Press, 1987), p. 13; emphasis in original.

[8] Altman, *American Musical Film*, p. 13.

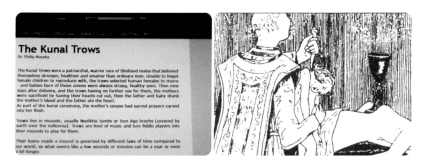

Figure 1 The Google search into local lore and pictures depicting the central sacrifice

Source: *Sacrifice*, directed by Peter A. Dowling (Subotica, 2016).

moves to the remote Shetland island long inhabited by her husband's family, only to discover that their difficulties having a baby and their plans for adoption are enmeshed with island folklore about the 'Kunal Trows', folklore that involves the ritual sacrifice of new mothers and the exchange of babies. Indeed, Bolton wrote that the legend of the Kunal Trows was the 'starting point, in *Sacrifice*': after she discovered 'the old Shetland legend of the Kunal Trows', she asked herself 'if I could make it the basis of a modern crime novel'.[9] Like Bolton, Tora goes through the same discovery of 'the old Shetland legend', one in which she realises she is already entrapped – and the 'old' is critical, as is the woodcut images she discovers that illuminate the 'old' legend. The 'modern', professional woman is set against a surviving ritual explicitly cast as 'ancient'. Bolton is perhaps an outlier in grounding her novel in a 'real' folk tale, although the category of 'real' folklore is inherently blurry, and Bolton's own fictionalising inevitably moves her away from that 'real. Much folk horror and Folk Gothic, on the other hand, explicitly invents its own folklore – what Dylan Foster and Jeffrey Tolbert have called the 'folkloresque' – that is the 'sense of folklore' or 'invented folklore' embedded in popular culture.[10] The folkloresque draws its power from its perceived 'authenticity', even as it is either partly or wholly 'invented'.[11] Whether 'real' or invented, though, diegetic

---

[9] Sharon Bolton, Personal correspondence (email), 16 January 2020.

[10] Michael Dylan Foster and Jeffrey A. Tolbert (eds.), *The Folkloresque: Reframing Folklore in a Popular Culture World* (Logan, UT: Utah State University Press, 2015), pp. 4, 126. See also Jeffrey A. Tolbert, 'The Frightening Folk: An Introduction to the Folkloresque in Horror', in Dawn Keetley and Ruth Heholt (eds.), *Folk Horror: New Global Pathways* (Cardiff: University of Wales Press, 2023), pp. 25–41, which discusses the folkloresque specifically in relation to folk horror (pp. 34–7).

[11] Tolbert, 'Frightening Folk', p. 34. See Mikel Koven's important analysis of the 'folkloristic fallacy' in Robin Hardy's *The Wicker Man*. Mikel J. Koven, *Film, Folklore, and Urban Legends* (Lanham, MD: The Scarecrow Press, 2008), pp. 25–35.

folklore positioned as expressly anachronistic is a defining characteristic of both folk horror and the Folk Gothic.

Along with folklore, the 'folk' form an equally critical component of folk horror and the Folk Gothic. In the history of folkloristics (the academic discipline of folklore), both the 'folk' and their lore emerged in the nineteenth century as signifiers of the past, of tradition.[12] Folklore scholars agree that from the late nineteenth through much of the twentieth century, the term signified what Simon Bronner calls the 'survival' of 'primitive' or 'savage' people into the 'civilised' modern era.[13] The 'folk' ensured the 'survival', as Paul Cowdell puts it, 'of ancient traditions'.[14] Such definitions of the usually static 'folk' were necessarily cast against a defining modern, enlightened and typically upwardly mobile 'normality'. As Stacey McDowell writes, '[t]raditionally, the "folk" have been equated with the lower classes, whose superstitions were regarded as naïve or "backward" in comparison to normative standards'.[15] James Thurgill elaborates that the 'folk' is a category grounded in 'perceived division in social classes, specifically between the burgeoning "mainstream" of the middle classes and working rural communities: the "folk"'.[16] In contemporary folkloristics, this notion of the primitive, rural or 'lower-class' 'folk' and their arcane lore has been superseded by the current reigning scholarly consensus in folklore studies that 'we are all folk', and that we all engage all the time in the process of shaping 'lore'.[17] Folk horror and the Folk Gothic, however, intentionally activate *obsolete* notions of 'folk'. As Jeffrey Tolbert aptly claims, the 'idea of anachronistic folk is central to folk horror', continuing that folk horror deploys views of the folk as 'hopelessly mired in a (putatively) traditional past'.[18] Far from the currently predominant notion that everyone is folk, then, the 'folk' in folk horror and Folk Gothic is marked – indeed, is *actively created* – as uniquely 'primitive', as

---

[12] As Raymond Williams describes it, the term 'folk-lore' was coined in 1846 by W. J. Thoms to articulate what was an ongoing understanding of lore as 'specialized to the past, with the associated senses of "traditional" or "legendary"'. The term served to concentrate 'the retrospective senses in both elements' – the 'folk' and the 'lore'. Raymond Williams, *Keywords: A Vocabulary of Culture and Society*, revised ed. (New York: Oxford University Press, 1985), p. 96.

[13] Simon J. Bronner (ed.), *The Meaning of Folklore: The Analytical Essays of Alan Dundes* (Logan, UT: Utah State University Press, 2007), pp. 54, 56, 67.

[14] Cowdell, '"Practising Witchcraft"', p. 304. Alan Dundes's seminal study of folklore also articulates how the 'folk' served to represent the 'uncivilized element of a civilized society', distinct from the entirely 'primitive' but nonetheless 'believed to have retained survivals of savagery'. Alan Dundes, *Interpreting Folklore* (Bloomington, IN: Indiana University Press, 1980), p. 2.

[15] Stacey McDowell, 'Folklore', in William Hughes, David Punter and Andrew Smith (eds.), *The Encyclopedia of the Gothic* (Malden, MA: Wiley-Blackwell, 2016), pp. 252–4 (p. 253).

[16] James Thurgill, 'The Fear of the Folk: On *Topophobia* and the Horror of Rural Landscapes', *Revenant: Critical and Creative Studies of the Supernatural*, 5 (2020): 33–56 (p. 42).

[17] See Bronner, *Meaning*, p. 54; and Tolbert, 'Frightening Folk', pp. 26–7, 28–9, 30.

[18] Tolbert, 'Frightening Folk', pp. 31, 33.

anomalous in its hewing to the 'old ways', and as distinct 'survivals' of the past into the present.[19]

The politics of representations of folklore and the folk in folk horror and Folk Gothic are fluid and multivalent. They can be seen, on the one hand, as a regressive exception to the movement towards a global cosmopolitan ethos of universal equity. Carina Hart describes this impulse through Svetlana Boym's notion of 'negative nostalgia', by which 'elements of the past that are now considered unacceptably retrograde are desired and revived' – and depicted, Hart adds, as 'dangerous'.[20] This 'danger' is levelled specifically at modern progressivism. On the other hand, folklore survivals and representations of the anachronistic 'folk' can be seen as a salutary impediment to the negative excesses of a homogenising modernity that seems bent on destroying local cultures: they represent the insistence of the local and the rooted in a global and rootless world.[21] As Paul Newland puts it, folk identities, based on enduring ancient practices, might well be represented as 'dark and disturbing', but they are also most definitely 'not governed and controlled by an increasingly global, glossy, homogeneous, superficial culture industry'.[22] Indeed, they are a bulwark against such forces – as are the folk horror and Folk Gothic texts that deploy these 'folk identities'. Manuel Aguirre has written of the convergence between folklore and the Gothic generally, arguing that part of the latter's 'function is the preservation of a fast-disappearing folklore'.[23] And indeed, both folk horror and Folk Gothic centre the struggle against an imminent sense of loss – the impending vanishing of the 'folk' and their lore. Folk horror and Folk Gothic often depict what Cal Flyn has called, in a slightly different context, 'islands of

---

[19] As part of his critique of folk horror's 'exoticizing' tendencies, Jamie Chambers argues that folk horror 'frequently ventriloquizes the subaltern rural community – partly referred, partly imagined – to forcibly cast it as a foil to the free agency, individualism, and progress of metropolitan life'. This is true, but I would argue that folk horror and Folk Gothic engage in the process for the most part self-consciously, not symptomatically. Chambers, 'Troubling Folk Horror', p. 18.

[20] Carina Hart, 'Gothic Folklore and Fairy Tale: Negative Nostalgia', *Gothic Studies*, 22:1 (2020): 1–13 (p. 4).

[21] Glennis Byron has likewise pointed out that, 'contemporary global Gothic increasingly appropriates and commodifies local or regional folklore'. Glennis Byron, 'Global Gothic', in David Punter (ed.), *A New Companion to the Gothic* (New York: Wiley-Blackwell, 2012), pp. 367–78 (p. 374). The conflict staged in both folk horror and the Folk Gothic can usefully be described as the conflict between what David Goodhart has called 'Anywhere' ideology – secular, mobile, rootless and global – and a competing 'Somewhere' worldview – traditional, rooted and local. David Goodhart, *The Road to Somewhere: The Populist Revolt and the Future of Politics* (London: Hurst, 2017), pp. 3–4.

[22] Newland, 'Folk Horror', p. 176.

[23] Manuel Aguirre, 'Gothic Fiction and Folk-Narrative Structure: The Case of Mary Shelley's *Frankenstein*', *Gothic Studies*, 15:2 (November 2013): 1–18 (p. 14).

abandonment',[24] local, 'primitive' communities left behind by the development of wealth and the migration of populations.

1.2 Folk Horror

While folk horror and Folk Gothic share a central expressly 'anachronistic' and often fabricated folklore and 'primitive' folk, they are also distinct literary and cinematic formations – beginning, of course, with the 'horror' of folk horror. Indeed, one of the reasons that the label 'folk horror' has been applied so promiscuously is because the 'horror' part of the label has been side-lined, a practice in line with a broader tendency to define 'horror' as loosely as possible and thus free it from its low-budget, exploitative and generally unsavoury associations. (This propensity is manifest most acutely in the twenty-first-century emergence of the variously dubbed 'elevated horror', 'prestige horror' and 'post-horror', and much folk horror has, not surprisingly, been swept into these categories as well.[25]) It is a central claim of this Element, though, that one of the reasons 'folk horror' is not an accurate designation for much of what has been labelled as such is that many purported 'folk horror' productions are not, in fact, very legible as 'horror'.

Perhaps, the definitive characteristic of horror is its central 'monster'. In his groundbreaking characterisation of 'art-horror', philosopher Noël Carroll argues that the presence of the monster demarcates horror from other genres, and he devotes significant space to elucidating the monster's two principal properties – that it is both threatening and impure. Elaborating on the critical concept of 'impurity', in particular, Carroll argues that the monster, as an impure being, 'is categorically interstitial, categorically contradictory, incomplete, or formless'. In their hybridity, in their existence on borders, monsters 'are not classifiable according to our standing categories'.[26] A second foundational definition of horror, by film critic Robin Wood, also centres a defining monster: horror is expressed by the deceptively simple formula, 'normality is threatened by the Monster'.[27] Horror's 'monsters', in Wood's articulation, are grounded in an opposing 'normality', the two forces inhabiting opposing sides of a clear boundary. Wood goes on to argue that the 'Monster' is the incarnation

---

[24] Cal Flyn, *Islands of Abandonment: Life in the Post-Human Landscape* (London: William Collins, 2021).

[25] See David Church, *Post-Horror: Art, Genre and Cultural Elevation* (Edinburgh: Edinburgh University Press, 2021). Not insignificantly, Church includes numerous films categorised as folk horror in his preliminary table of 'post-horror' films (p. 14).

[26] Noël Carroll, *The Philosophy of Horror; or, Paradoxes of the Heart* (New York: Routledge, 1990), pp. 32–3.

[27] Robin Wood, *Hollywood from Vietnam to Reagan* (New York: Columbia University Press, 1986), p. 78.

of everything that society – 'normality' – represses or oppresses, and that, through the monster, the horror film stages 'the struggle for recognition of all that our civilization represses or oppresses'.[28] Although Carroll's and Wood's definitions of horror are very different, articulating, respectively, a cognitive and a psychoanalytic framework, they are united in denoting the monster as a definitive characteristic of horror.

Implicit in Carroll's and Wood's discussions of the monstrous is another trait that is critical to horror: borders. As interstitial beings, monsters necessarily 'cross the boundaries of the deep categories of a culture's conceptual scheme'; they inevitably breach cultural categories.[29] Wood's formulation is predicated specifically on the border separating 'normality' and the repressed or oppressed 'monster', domains that are at the same time both necessarily demarcated and mutually constitutive ('normality' needs its 'monster' on the other side of that boundary, and vice versa). Borders and their inevitable transgression are thus central to both Carroll's and Wood's definitions of horror – the borders that demarcate the categories that structure 'normality' or the borders that serve to demarcate that 'normality' from what it strives to disavow and expel. As a result, geographical borders often loom large in horror narratives, serving to represent visually and narratively the violation of more intimate ontological and societal boundary crossings. As Stephen Prince astutely puts it, the horror film reiteratively 'involves the transgression of boundaries, the violation of the spatialized social system'.[30] Horror, then, stages the repeated crossing of borders that are only able to be transgressed because they exist in the first place.

Not surprisingly, folk horror is impelled by the crossing of borders, often manifest as a linear temporality – a movement forward through time and space. Some of the most memorable and exemplary scenes from folk horror involve movement through space, across borders: Sergeant Neil Howie's plane ride from the mainland of Scotland to Summerisle, for instance, or the journey of the Americans in *Midsommar* (Ari Aster, 2019) first by plane to Stockholm and then by car to the isolated community of Hälsingland, a journey that will carry them so far from what is familiar that Aster amplifies the breach in reality, and the disorienting crossing of cultural borders, by shooting a significant part of the drive upside down; when the camera rights itself and we see the road sign for Hälsingland, we also see a swerving tire track off the side of the road before that

---

[28] Wood, *Hollywood*, p. 75.   [29] Carroll, *Philosophy*, pp. 31–2, 33.

[30] Stephen Prince, 'Dread, Taboo, and *The Thing*: Toward a Social Theory of the Horror Film', in Stephen Prince (ed.), *The Horror Film* (New Brunswick, NJ: Rutgers University Press, 2004), pp. 118–30 (p. 125).

Figure 2 The boundary-crossing car journey from the USA to remote Sweden
Source: *Midsommar*, directed by Ari Aster (Square Peg, 2019).

particular boundary is crossed. The Americans fail to make such a swerve, instead crossing the border and sealing their fates (Figure 2).

Exemplary horror, folk horror specifically is defined by the violent encounter of characters who meet at a border (whether spatial, ontological or cognitive) demarcating on the one side a secular and 'normal' modernity and, on the other, an archaic and pagan 'monstrous' folk.[31] The very existence – and resurgence – of folk horror demonstrates the existence of profound divisions within the social terrains depicted within (and existing beyond) the text. Folk horror thrives on divisions of class, region, nation, race and religion. Adam Scovell has identified one of the four 'links' in the 'folk horror chain' as the 'skewed belief systems and morality' of the 'folk', typically an isolated community.[32] The descriptor 'skewed' only works, of course, because the narrative counterposes those 'belief systems and morality' deemed to be 'skewed' to a presumed 'normality'; it only works because of the presence of a border. The 'folk' are pushed towards the 'ontological liminality' of Carroll's 'monstrosity', moreover, by their devotion to the pagan – to the 'old ways' and to ancient rites, many of which blur the human/non-human divide, a blurring embodied in masks and costumes. Sometimes the rites of the 'folk' are disclosed as actually enmeshed in the

---

[31] It should be added that, in folk horror, both the (modern, secular, urban, global) protagonists and the (primitive, pagan, rural, local) antagonists tend to presume that *they* represent normality and that the *other* is the 'monster', although the film typically puts this certainty in doubt. In the end, though, while the roles of 'normality' and 'monstrous' are often troubled in folk horror, even inverted, they nonetheless persist, and their persistence is a hallmark of folk *horror*. See Keetley, 'Defining', pp. 10–15.

[32] Scovell, *Folk Horror*, p. 18.

supernatural, and a literal 'monster' is conjured up – as in *The Blood on Satan's Claw*, with its rising of 'Behemoth' at the film's culminating ritual, or in David Bruckner's *The Ritual* (2017), in which the 'monstrous' tribe inhabiting the forest of Sweden perform sacrifices to an unearthly and incarnate deity who appears at the end to claim its ritual victim. Much of the time, however, the boundary-crossing 'monster' is the 'folk' themselves.

Horror, and thus folk horror, are also necessarily characterised by bodily threat, shock and violence. Of the four links in Scovell's 'folk horror chain', it is the last one, 'the resulting action from this skewed social consciousness with all of its horrific fallout', that most often pushes narratives into 'horror' terrain.[33] Scovell goes on to add that the 'summoning' or 'happening' is violent, 'primal and raw', and 'is often about death in the slowest, most ritualistic of ways'.[34] Indeed, the narrative trajectory of most folk horror is towards a violent and sacrificial death: the burning of Neil Howie in *The Wicker Man*; the ritualistic battle that Jay (Neil Maskell) is forced into at the end of Ben Wheatley's *Kill List* (2011) that ends up with his killing his wife and son; the violent sacrifice of Dom (Sam Troughton), impaled on a tree by the deity Jötunn at the end of *The Ritual*; and the burning alive of several sacrificial victims, including the American Christian (Jack Reynor) in a bear skin, at the end of *Midsommar*. Scovell's use of the term 'summoning' is apt in that folk horror texts are infused with the sense of impending violence, as the protagonists are lured – from the beginning – into plots that bend them to this narrative end. From its beginning, folk horror is freighted with its culminating violence.

1.3 Folk Gothic

Through the modifier 'folk', Folk Gothic obviously shares with folk horror its deployment (and frequent fabrication) of diegetic folklore along with the presence of the 'folk' and an abiding sense of their imminent vanishing. Folk Gothic does not share folk horror's incarnate monsters, its forward impetus across spatial and ontological boundaries and the shock and repulsion elicited through its bodily violence. While some critics have already acknowledged the thematic interconnections of the Gothic and folklore,[35] what I argue here is that Folk Gothic is defined by particular temporal and spatial relations that serve to

---

[33] Scovell, *Folk Horror*, pp. 17–18. [34] Scovell, *Folk Horror*, p. 18.

[35] See Mark A. Vieira, *Hollywood Horror: From Gothic to Cosmic* (New York: Harry N. Abrams, 2003), who ties pre-1968 Gothic cinema to folklore, writing that the Gothic refers to 'films whose horror springs from the folklore of Central Europe' – a definition that expressly mixes Gothic, horror, and folklore (p. 7). In her introduction to a special issue of *Gothic Studies* on gothic and folklore, Hart highlights 'folkloric figures' such as 'vampires, witches, werewolves, ghosts and doppelgängers'. Hart, 'Gothic Folklore', pp. 3, 5, 12.

shape non-human stories; these stories tilt towards land and objects and a consequent loosening of anthropocentrism. Folk horror and Folk Gothic may share the 'folk', but the Folk Gothic self-consciously conjures the 'folk' only to erode its presence. In its emphasis on particular temporal and spatial relations – *not* on literal 'folk' and 'monsters' – the Folk Gothic unfurls stories outside of what Eileen Joy has dubbed the typical 'human-centred, historicist frames of reference'.[36] When non-human things and forces, the natural and built environments, move to the fore, conventional stories and plots begin to falter and change. Time and space become unloosed from human time and space, entering a much more impersonal Folk Gothic time and space.

First and foremost, the temporality of the Folk Gothic is in stark contrast to that of folk horror. While the time of 'horror' tends to be linear, a relentless movement forward (albeit often towards a sacrificial fate long in the planning), the Gothic plot is predicated on recursive time. Chris Baldick's influential definition of the Gothic articulates a crucial characteristic of the genre as 'a fearful sense of *inheritance in time*'.[37] The 'inheritance in time' of the traditional Gothic is often familial (the family sin, the curse passed from father to son), even as the familial connects to the broadly societal (the visiting on future generations of the past sins of slavery, racism and capitalist expansion, for instance). As Anne Williams has described the Gothic: 'All these tales [are] about the power of the past (especially the deeds of one's ancestors) to affect the present'.[38] In Folk Gothic as a literary and cinematic form, however, the Gothic's recursivity is bound up not with 'the deeds of one's ancestors' but with the reiterative patterns of a more anonymous folklore: the Folk Gothic is constituted by tales passed from one generation to another and serving to bind a particular group together, whether it be a village, a tribe, or a nation. But these tales are always transmitted in specific localised communities, and so, beneath the community is inevitably the place – and in Folk Gothic, the communities that inherit the repeated lore often dissolve into the landscape that grounds it.

Particular spatial relations are thus also crucial to the Folk Gothic. Baldick continues his definition of the traditional Gothic by writing that it combines 'inheritance in time' with 'a claustrophobic sense of *enclosure in space*, these two dimensions reinforcing each other to produce an impression of sickening descent into disintegration'.[39] The space of Folk Gothic is almost never those

---

[36] Eileen A. Joy, 'Weird Reading', *Speculations: A Journal of Speculative Realism*, 4 (2013): 28–34 (p. 29).

[37] Chris Baldick, 'Introduction', in Chris Baldick (ed.), *The Oxford Book of Gothic Tales* (New York: Oxford University Press, 1993), pp. xi–xxiii (p. xix; emphasis added).

[38] Anne Williams, *Art of Darkness: A Poetics of Gothic* (Chicago, IL: University of Chicago Press, 1995), p. 90.

[39] Baldick, 'Introduction', p. xix; emphasis added.

oppressive interiors common to the Gothic – castles, abbeys, cellars and attics. Instead, the space of Folk Gothic is exterior, 'natural'; it is the land itself, although 'nature' is never as free from human involvement as it may seem. Indeed, the non-human landscapes of Folk Gothic are necessarily imbricated with human lore, with history and myth, and with the places and artefacts of ritual. The entrapping sense of 'enclosure' in Folk Gothic, then is not exerted by walls – far from it. It comes from land in which the reiterative force of folkloric tales is rooted (sometimes literally). In contrast to the multiple forms of border crossing in folk horror, Folk Gothic is about the vertiginous realisation of being already trapped – of circling, returning – in a very particular place.

In the Folk Gothic, the presence of ritual often serves to crystallise the ways in which characters find themselves in a recursive time and an entrapping place, both of which accrue a power that overwhelms human choice and will. Agency is granted instead to non-human forces, to forces that are specific to the land itself and to rituals that involve individuals but that increasingly are represented as having a power all their own. Indeed, as Barry Stephenson has claimed, ritual inherently serves as 'an actor in its own right'. It has 'force, power, efficacy, or agency'. An action becomes more like ritual precisely to the degree that individual intention is attenuated and, as Stephenson puts it, 'it receives spatial and temporal framing'.[40] Ritual thus converges with the structuring of the Folk Gothic not around individual actors but through entrapping spatial and temporal networks. The 'handing over of agency is the core quality of the ritual frame', Stephenson writes.[41] It is also the core quality of the Folk Gothic.

Algernon Blackwood's 1908 story, 'Ancient Sorceries', serves as exemplary Folk Gothic precisely in its centring ritual as 'spatial and temporal framing' that erodes everything human. A man named Arthur Vezin, traveling across Northern France, is compelled by the hordes of tourists to get off the train at an isolated village that straggles up a mountain and is 'crowned by the twin towers' of a 'ruined cathedral'. Once off the train, Vezin finds he has 'stepped clean out of modern life into a bygone century'.[42] He discovers a village in thrall to the 'spell of the past', one rooted in the land itself: the town grew out of a hill 'as naturally as an ancient wood' (p. 93). The more time he spends in the village, the more Vezin finds himself unable to make decisions, and he feels 'trapped and powerless to escape', caught in the 'web' woven by the town – and by two

---

[40] Barry Stephenson, *Ritual: A Very Short Introduction* (New York: Oxford University Press, 2015), pp. 70–1, 77.

[41] Stephenson, *Ritual*, p. 84.

[42] Algernon Blackwood, 'Ancient Sorceries', in Sunand Tryambak Joshi (ed.), *Ancient Sorceries and Other Weird Tales* (New York: Penguin, 2002), pp. 87–130 (p. 90); subsequent references will be included parenthetically in the text.

women in particular, an older woman and her daughter Ilsé (p. 102). As the story progresses, Vezin feels increasingly driven by 'impulses he scarcely recognised as his own', and this loss of agency, of self, which he connects to Ilsé, fills him with dread (pp. 108, 107, 103). At the climax of the story, Vezin finds himself caught in the ritual of the village's Witches' Sabbath, a night when 'Things were on the move everywhere'. This night, markedly defined by a repeated ritual that can happen only in this place and by a stirring of 'Things', signals the apex of the village's effect on Vezin, its overcoming of his distinct subjectivity (p. 120). Even as Vezin feels estranged from his 'self', however, he feels at the same time that the ritual of the Witches' Sabbath is 'familiar': 'It had all happened before just so, hundreds of times, and he himself had taken part in it and known the wild madness of it all' (p. 121). Vezin is trapped in this repeated rite in this isolated village, one marked by the power of 'Things' that take on their own force and wrench away his very sense of having an individual 'self' at all.

At the very last moment, Vezin is able to pull himself away from this reiterated ritual and from the place where his ancestors, it turns out, had been burned at the stake as witches hundreds of years ago. He extracts himself from this 'vivid revival' that is endlessly repeated – a veritable 'vortex of forces arising out of the intense activities of a past life' (pp. 128, 130). As the physician to whom Vezin eventually recounts his story concludes, Vezin had retained enough 'recognition' to 'fight against the degradation of returning, even in memory, to a former and lower state of development' (p. 130). Vezin ultimately, but barely, escapes the interwoven force of particular place, an organic community bound together by cyclical and primitive rites, those reiterated rituals themselves, and the 'things' that 'were on the move everywhere'. And Blackwood is explicit about the ways that, in this place, Vezin loses the ability to choose, to make decisions, even to maintain 'the Self I knew' (p. 103). Instead, impersonal forces – specifically, the temporal and spatial relations of the Folk Gothic – take over.

As Blackwood articulates with his 'Things were on the move everywhere', agentic 'things' are central to Folk Gothic. Objects have long featured in discussion of the Gothic: 'the enchanted artifact', McDowell writes, is a recurring 'element' of the Gothic.[43] In Folk Gothic, the Gothic's general preoccupation with objects intersects with an 'item-oriented' approach to folklore: the objects of Folk Gothic are, specifically, folkloric items that embody local, collective traditions – things such as historical artefacts and stones, ancient books and paintings. The Folk Gothic's exploitation of an 'item-oriented' folkloristics aligns with the way in

---

[43] McDowell, p. 253. For more on the importance of objects and 'things' to the Gothic, see Chapter 3.

which both folk horror and Folk Gothic integrate the 'folk' and their lore into their narratives in highly anachronistic ways. Thus, in the Folk Gothic, folklore is distinctly not what contemporary folkloristics claims it is – the domain of everyone, all the time, including in highly mediated spaces. Indeed, the emphasis of folkloristics on 'item-oriented folklore' – on antiquities – is an approach rooted in the past and only persists, when it does, in popular (not scholarly) understandings of folklore.[44] Elliott Oring, for instance, has described a 'long tradition of antiquarian scholarship' that focused 'upon anything old: old buildings, old legal documents, old artefacts, old tales, old songs, old customs'. The 'distant past' and a vanishing 'peasantry' was preserved, folklorists asserted, in their objects – in a 'collection of things'.[45] Or, as Roger D. Abrahams describes it, in 'dislocated items and objects in time and space' and in 'bounded items'.[46] Abrahams connects this practice of charting 'the path of dissemination of items or objects across time and space' to what he calls a 'Romantic' theory of cultural production 'that continually derogates the present in the pursuit of an authentic past'.[47] And, indeed, the ubiquity in Folk Gothic of 'items' and 'objects' as synecdochic for the broader traditions of the 'folk' does represent the effort to create such an 'authentic past' and its powerful grasp on the present, a power vested precisely in folkloric objects that accrue the agency of Gothic things.

My approach to the Folk Gothic joins the focus of both the Gothic and folkloristics on objects with a new materialism that expressly accounts for the agency of 'things'. Summarising Bill Brown's 'Thing Theory', Lisa Mullen helpfully articulates his distinction 'between intransigent things and obedient objects'.[48] Folkloric objects, which in the Folk Gothic evolve into deeply unsettling folkloric 'things', profoundly challenge what Brown calls the 'dialectic by which human subjects and inanimate objects may be said to constitute one another'.[49] Brown draws a sharp distinction between the reassuring 'obedient objects' that constitute recognisable humans and the 'intransigent things' that profoundly destabilise the human subject. Indeed, Brown claims that 'things' emerge – that we confront the 'thingness of objects' – precisely when they 'stop working for us'. The 'story of objects asserting themselves as things', he continues, 'is the story of a changed

---

44 Tolbert, 'Frightening Folk', pp. 28–9.
45 Elliott Oring, 'On the Concepts of Folklore', in Elliott Oring (ed.), *Folk Groups and Folklore Genres: An Introduction* (Logan, UT: Utah State University Press, 1986), pp. 1–22 (pp. 6, 18).
46 Roger D. Abrahams, 'Phantoms of Romantic Nationalism in Folkloristics', *The Journal of American Folklore*, 106:419 (Winter 1993): 3–37 (pp. 20, 31).
47 Abrahams, 'Phantoms', p. 19.
48 Lisa Mullen, *Mid-Century Gothic: The Uncanny Objects of Modernity in British Literature and Culture after the Second World War* (Manchester: Manchester University Press, 2019), p. 10.
49 Bill Brown, 'The Tyranny of Things (Trivia in Karl Marx and Mark Twain)', *Critical Inquiry*, 28:2 (Winter 2002): 442–69 (p. 446).

relation to the human subject'.[50] This is the 'thing-power' that Jane Bennett has so powerfully articulated – a theory that seeks 'to attend to the it as actant'.[51] Mullen has recently approached the 'things' of the Gothic from a new materialistic perspective, taking up mid-twentieth-century consumer goods, 'objects invested with economic and cultural power'. She has drawn attention to the ways in which the Gothic 'return of repressed enchantment' worked to animate objects as things, 'highlighting the auratic autonomy of newly re-mythologised objects'.[52] The folkloric 'things' of Folk Gothic, however, are not those objects or even 'things' of rampant economic consumerism that Mullen explores; in fact, they can serve as powerful stays against the cultural dominance of both capitalism and consumerism. Folk Gothic 'things' are not up for exchange in the market. Their value, meaning and power lie emphatically elsewhere, as they offer an alternative to a life lived entwined with consumer goods. With its 'things' that are integral to – constitutive of – folkloric stories and rituals, the Folk Gothic reanimates the inert 'items', artefacts' or 'objects' of antiquarian study, recasting them as 'things' that exert an autonomous meaning and power within folkloric narratives, a power that overwhelms individual human agency and embeds it in less visible forms of non-human agency.

The centrality of folkloric objects in the Folk Gothic extends the propensity of critics to define the Gothic through accretions of reiterated tropes (e.g., castles, abbeys, graveyards, persecuted heroines, tyrannical patriarchs).[53] The tropes of Folk Gothic are the particular 'things' that serve to carry the meanings of folklore, and the close visual and narrative attention to these artefacts shapes a particular aesthetic for the Folk Gothic, one that highlights detailed descriptions (in fiction) and tight visual close-ups (in film and television); these descriptions and shots emphasise foreground over background, close-ups over long shots, detail over scale, the proximate over the remote.[54] The textual passages and visual shots that capture Folk Gothic are isolating, atomising; they appear to disrupt familiar time, orientation in space, and narrative flow. As the narrative unfolds, however, the objects captured in narrative and visual detail reveal occluded and unfamiliar aspects of time, space, and agency, all of

---

[50] Bill Brown, 'Thing Theory', *Critical Inquiry*, 28:1 (Autumn 2001): 1–22 (p. 4).

[51] Jane Bennett, *Vibrant Matter: A Political Ecology of Things* (Durham, NC: Duke University Press, 2010), p. 3.

[52] Mullen, *Mid-Century Gothic*, p. 9.

[53] Aldana Reyes, for instance, has pointed out that the Gothic has enduringly been 'identifiable at the level of surface', through visual motifs and tropes – and, paramount among them, he reiterates are 'grandiose architecture', 'haunted castles', the 'castle or mansion on a promontory' and 'imposing castles'. Xavier Aldana Reyes, *Gothic Cinema* (New York: Routledge, 2020), pp. 9, 14, 16, 18.

[54] See Keetley, '*True Detective*'s Folk Gothic', pp. 132–5.

which impinge on the characters. A central tenet of Folk Gothic, that folkloric 'things' *determine* their characters, is represented textually and visually, then, in their aesthetic foregrounding. Indeed, it is important to emphasise that Folk Gothic 'things' are not used figuratively – to reveal something about human characters. Gothic 'things' are agents and forces in their own right, and while human characters may certainly strive to render those objects meaningful in their own terms, those objects escape that imposed narrative and have their own power in the world.

The centrality of archaic 'folk' and lore within Folk Gothic orients us to a different notion of the uncanny than that which has dominated scholarship on the Gothic. Freud famously claimed that while one source of the uncanny derives from individual repression, another is 'when primitive beliefs that have been *surmounted* appear to be once again confirmed'.[55] As Ken Gelder aptly puts it, 'Freud comes to a conclusion which stands with one foot in the psyche and the other in ethnography and folklore studies'.[56] McDowell notes that folklore has a specifically 'uncanny familiarity', the sense of 'having been heard before without the listener's ever knowing quite where – an echo of something one was not aware of having originally heard'. In this way, McDowell continues, Gothic that is predicated on folklore 'unnervingly revives the past' in ways that activate Freud's notion of the uncanny as the intrusion into lived experience of 'surmounted primitive beliefs'.[57] Scholarship on the Gothic has devoted much more time to exploring the uncanniness that derives from individual and societal repression than to the uncanniness that derives from the (only seemingly) 'surmounted primitive beliefs'. The latter is front and centre in the Folk Gothic, however, as it repeatedly depicts modern and 'enlightened' characters discovering that those 'primitive beliefs' structure entire communities, that they are rooted in particular landscapes and objects, transmitted through folklore and have by no means been 'surmounted'. What Hart calls the 'resurrection of folkloric terrors'[58] may be a new experience for the rootless, global characters of Folk Gothic, but it is the lived reality for the 'folk' they encounter. Folk Gothic thus mobilises a particular form of the uncanny – the folkloric uncanny – which depicts the often-terrifying encounter of 'modern' characters with persistent 'primitive beliefs'.

If folk horror's principal affect is a shock and repulsion based on graphic bodily violence, the principal affect of the Folk Gothic is dread. Cynthia

---

[55] Sigmund Freud, *The Uncanny*, trans. David McLintock (New York: Penguin, 2003), p. 155. For others who mention this aspect of the uncanny, see McDowell, 'Folklore', p. 253, and Hart, 'Gothic Folklore', p. 6.

[56] Ken Gelder, *Reading the Vampire* (New York: Routledge, 1994), p. 44.

[57] McDowell, 'Folklore', p. 253.   [58] Hart, 'Gothic Folklore', p. 6.

Freeland has aptly defined dread as an 'encounter with something terrible or unsettling that is also deep, obscure, and difficult to comprehend. There may be hints of a terrifying agent out there', she continues, 'but it need not be a repulsive monster', and, indeed, it 'can remain uncertain whether there is *any* agent involved in the threat at all'. Dread is, she adds, a response 'to things that are deeply unnerving for no clear reason'.[59] In distinguishing what induces dread from the 'repulsive monster' at the heart of horror, Freeland makes the critical point that, in narratives predicated on dread, there may not be any clear 'agent' at all.[60] The Folk Gothic does indeed, I argue, raise profound questions about agency – and these questions serve to draw a line demarcating folk horror, with its discernible monsters (human and supernatural), from the Folk Gothic, in which agency is wrested from the human and its monsters and dispersed through the non-human. In Folk Gothic, agency is immanent in the landscape and in folkloric 'things' and in the uncanny power of interwoven inherited ritual and tradition – all of which foreground inexorably repetitive patterns over human lives and communities.

Freeland's articulation of dread tellingly implies the centrality of objects. She writes that dread is a 'response to *things* that are deeply unnerving for no clear reason', and she then offers *things* as examples: the bundles of twigs hanging from trees in *The Blair Witch Project*, curtainless windows in *The Others* and open kitchen cupboards in *Sixth Sense*.[61] We can indeed, as Freeland continues, sense that '*something* is wrong in such scenes', but whereas Freeland adds, 'without knowing why',[62] I would add that it is precisely the foregrounding of the 'things' she describes that drives dread, that insinuates that feeling that, yes, some *thing* is wrong. The Folk Gothic's 'non-human' – the autonomous and self-perpetuating drive of tradition and ritual, the power of places and things that are imbued with meanings that surpass individual grasp – serves to dislodge the typical anthropocentric frame of narrative, rendering the Folk Gothic a literary and filmic terrain that eludes familiar human-centred narratives and that thus, for this very reason, induces dread.

Folkloristics has long identified the tension between a 'folk' that *uses* ritual and tradition to control uncontrollable forces in their lives and a folk who are, paradoxically, more or less *controlled by* the ritual and tradition by which they seek to control those uncontrollable forces. Indeed, this conflict exploits the tension in folkloristics between the idea of an active 'folk' choosing and adapting traditions and a passive 'folk' 'following' tradition.[63] While the

---

[59] Cynthia Freeland, 'Horror and Art-Dread', in Stephen Prince (ed.), *The Horror Film* (New York: Routledge, 2004), pp. 189–205 (p. 193); emphasis in original.
[60] Freeland, 'Horror', p. 193.   [61] Freeland, 'Horror', p. 193; emphasis added.
[62] Freeland, 'Horror', p. 193; emphasis in original.   [63] Bronner, *Folklore*, p. 20.

main current of folklore scholarship has rightly emphasised the former under-standing of the folk as always and everywhere active participants in the creation of meaning, Folk Gothic (even more than folk horror) hews to the anachronistic conception of the folk as subject to ritual, to agentic folkloric 'artefacts' and to the land in which they are by definition rooted. As the indwelling force of ritual and tradition, of thing and land, comes to the fore, the Folk Gothic unfurls stories outside of anthropocentrism.

2 From Horror to Folk Gothic

The Descent, The Green Inferno, Midsommar, The Ritual, Pet Sematary, In the Earth

This section explains the structural differences between folk horror and Folk Gothic not by defining two absolutely separate categories but by describing six films that lie on a continuum from folk horror to Folk Gothic, thus illuminating not only the stark differences at the edges but also the shared ground in between. Those films are *The Descent* (Neil Marshall, 2005), *The Green Inferno* (Eli Roth, 2013), *Midsommar* (Ari Aster, 2019), *The Ritual* (David Bruckner, 2017), *Pet Sematary* (Mary Lambert, 1989) and *In the Earth* (Ben Wheatley, 2021). All six of these films share a similar plot, one that has become one of the most easily identifiable markers of 'folk horror': a group of young people marked as urban, modern, secular, multicultural and global travel to a world that is none of these things. What transpires in each film as this plot unfurls serves to distinguish folk horror from Folk Gothic. The principal marker of this difference, I argue, is the gradual displacement of humans and human agency in the Folk Gothic. Folk Gothic embodies the depersonalisation implicit in Chris Baldick's influential definition of the Gothic, the grammatical construction of which (specifically the erasure of human subjects) signals the way in which time and space emerge as powerful actors in the Gothic: there is 'an inheritance in time' and an 'enclosure in space'. These 'dimensions', which are the actors in this formulation, reinforce each other 'to produce an impression of sickening descent into disintegration'.[64] In the Gothic, then, the impersonal 'dimensions' of time and space move to the foreground. In Folk Gothic specifically, the 'survivals' of folklore and folk practices and ritual – the 'old ways' – ultimately displace human actors and intent, as does the environment – the non-human objects and land that have persisted long before and will persist long after any individual human or commu-nity. It is these rituals, these objects and this land, that exert the uncanny force that drives the Folk Gothic plot, superseding the will of human characters.

---

[64] Baldick, 'Introduction', p. xix.

2.1 The Descent

The first three films on this continuum demonstrate the contours of folk horror, moving inward from its far reaches (*The Descent* and *The Green Inferno*) towards what is arguably one of the genre's exemplars (*Midsommar*). I begin with Neil Marshall's *The Descent* because it is a near-perfect embodiment of a straight-up 'horror' film while nonetheless offering seeds of folk horror. It tells the story of six friends who travel from to the Appalachian Mountains of North Carolina for a spelunking expedition in what turns out to be an unexplored cave system. The friends descend into the cave, crossing the border that separates the familiar aboveground world from the unknown belowground terrain. One by one, they are attacked and killed by the mute and cannibalistic creatures that inhabit the caves. These creatures perfectly embody Noël Carroll's 'impure' monsters: they are 'categorically interstitial, categorically contradictory', 'not classifiable according to our standing categories'; they resemble the human (barely) but are also completely 'other' – blind, deathly white and cannibalistic.[65] *The Descent* is thus exemplary horror with its crossing of both spatial and ontological boundaries, with its hybrid and threatening 'monsters', denizens of a dark terrain beneath the familiar world. The film revels, moreover, in gore – in broken bones piercing skin, in bodies ripped up and devoured. And it activates almost all of the evolutionary fears on Mathias Clasen's list of fears that are exploited in horror, fears that are hard-wired and instilled by millennia of conditioning: blood, darkness, sudden loud noises, looming objects, heights, closed-in spaces, deep water, predators and, of course, 'the sudden, unmotivated appearance of a monster' – a monster intent on consuming you.[66]

Iconic horror, *The Descent* nonetheless also gestures to folk horror, not least in its structuring conflict between the modern/urban/global and the primitive/rural/local. The six friends, all outfitted with cutting-edge caving and orienting equipment, are from far-flung parts of the globe. This cosmopolitan group – none of them native to Appalachia – are expressly tourists; this is absolutely not a place they (would) live. The characters' central act of 'invasion' – of descent (a first descent before the descent into the cave) – is emphasised by the multitude of aerial shots of their cars as they penetrate unfamiliar terrain, crossing borders that are visually reiterated by tree lines, rivers and roads. These shots are staples of the folk horror genre, and *The Descent* draws in particular on the long scenes of the main characters' drive from the city to rural

---

[65] Carroll, *Philosophy*, pp. 32–3.
[66] Mathias Clasen, *Why Horror Seduces* (New York: Oxford University Press, 2017), pp. 32, 36, 37, 40, 42.

Appalachia early in John Boorman's *Deliverance* (1972), a film that itself inhabits the outer margins of folk horror.

That the unfamiliar terrain entered by the cosmopolitan protagonists of *The Descent* is 'primitive' is emphasised by the eventual appearance of the cave dwellers, the 'crawlers'. While they are visually monstrous, they *resemble* the human. Indeed, director Neil Marshall has stated that they are 'the cavemen who stayed in the cave'. They are 'an offshoot of the human race',[67] but an offshoot that does not in fact exist – a monstrous imagining of what humans *might* have been if they had evolved for millennia underground. This conflict between modern 'intruders' and 'primitive' cave dwellers is amplified by the 'primitive' nature of the cave system itself. It has never been named or mapped, and thus it doubly represents the inherently primal nature of the cave as Antonio Sanna has described it: 'the return to the cave implies a flight from contemporary life towards a more simple experience of life and nature'. The journey into an unmapped cave thus inherently limns the core journey of folk horror, which can be articulated through Sanna's words: a 'flight from contemporary life towards a more simple experience'.[68] That the crawlers inhabit the 'primal' cave only amplifies their status as archaic 'survivals', in stark contrast to the mobile women with their global and portable identities and their modern technologies. The primal resonances of both cave and crawlers are intensified still further by the fact that the crawlers visually merge with the inorganic rock, truly stuck in place.

In an intriguing albeit fleeting reading, James Marriott interprets *The Descent* through a colonialist paradigm, which itself provocatively maps onto the central structuring conflict of folk horror – between the mobile cosmopolitan outsider and the rooted and 'archaic' local. As Lorenzo Veracini puts it, the colonialist framework 'emphasises the antagonisms pitting colonising metropole and colonial periphery',[69] an apt description of the plot of *The Descent* in which mostly British women descend on rural Appalachia. In describing what he takes to be their combined British, Scandinavian and Eurasian origins, Marriott writes, more specifically, that the women form 'a fairly accurate representation of early immigrant cultures in the US'. He then adds that the crawlers could represent 'the indigenous people of the US', cast within a 'colonial framework' as 'savage, alien and prolific, protecting their environment from interlopers'.[70]

---

[67] Marshall quoted in James Marriott, *The Descent* (Leighton Buzzard: Auteur 2013), p. 43.

[68] Antonio Sanna, 'A "New" Environment for the Horror Film: The Cave as Negation of Postmodernity and Globalization', *Journal of Film and Video*, 65:4 (Winter 2013): 17–24 (p. 24).

[69] Lorenzo Veracini, *Settler Colonialism: A Theoretical Overview* (London: Palgrave Macmillan, 2010), p. 5.

[70] Marriott, *Descent*, p. 45.

Marriott's description thus makes it clear that the plot of the global outsider confronting the 'local' and the 'primitive' can be mobilised within the colonialist paradigm. Nathaniel Budzinski has pointed out that, read through the colonialist lens, folk horror almost always adopts the perspective of the dominant culture, of the 'outsider looking in; the camera's eye making us spectators arriving in a strange land, encountering its strange inhabitants with their strange tribal rites'.[71] That folk horror maps so well onto the colonialist paradigm, specifically, taking the perspective of the outsider or 'colonising metropole', is in large part what makes it 'horror'. After all, it is this very colonising perspective that inevitably shapes 'monsters' out of those who inhabit the 'colonised periphery', that 'strange land'.

As much as *The Descent* evokes folk horror in its central narrative conflict, suggesting its potential colonialist meanings, it finally strays from the specifically *folk* horror remit in that it does not discernibly embed its antagonists in a folkloristic tradition. There is only one scene that arguably represents the mute crawlers as a potential 'community' capable of transmitting 'culture' – and that is a scene in which the women discover a cave painting that depicts the crawlers' livelihood (animals) and their means of getting in and out of their cave. In the end, though, these paintings form the very barest evidence of 'lore' – of nascent tradition and ritual; they are too 'primitive', too inchoate, to bestow on the crawlers the status of the antagonistic community of folk horror (although they lie adjacent to it). The crawlers persist instead as the 'monsters' of horror, representing a more primordial threat. As Rich Johnson writes in a review of *The Descent*, 'trolls, troglodytes and any other form of cave dweller are a dehumanized or devolved concept. The imagery conjured from these catacombs evokes a fearful place that connects us all to our primordial nature'.[72] In the end, *The Descent* features creatures of 'primordial' (human) nature in a metaphoric primordial space (the cave) – *not* a 'primitive' human community.

While it does not grant its antagonists their own folklore, the central plot of *The Descent* does tap into the early folklore studies paradigm that has driven folk horror – that the primitive communities so central to folk horror are 'survivals' of past traditions in the present.[73] The film stages not only a clash between modern and archaic but also between present and past, a past very

---

[71] Nathaniel Budzinski, '"It's All an Indian Burial Ground": Folk Horror Cinema's Reckoning with Colonial Violence', *ArtReview*, 10 December 2021, https://artreview.com/its-all-an-indian-burial-ground-folk-horror-cinema-reckoning-with-colonial-violence/ [last accessed 15 April 2023].

[72] Rich Johnson, 'Dungeons Deep and Caverns Old – Revisiting Neil Marshall's The Descent', *Fangoria*, 30 April 2021, www.fangoria.com/original/revisiting-the-descent/ [last accessed 15 April 2023].

[73] Cowdell, '"Practising Witchcraft"', pp. 298, 304.

much alive *in* the present. Indeed, the existence of alternative evolutionary branches of the human, as Marriott points out, is a concept often 'explored in folklore, fantastic fiction – think of Arthur Machen's "little people"'.[74] Establishing an adjacency to folk horror, *The Descent* both performs an obsolete folkloristics – its plot animates past 'survivals' in the present – as well as offering up a traditional folklore tale – the discovery of an offshoot evolutionary branch of the human.[75]

2.2 The Green Inferno

Eli Roth's *The Green Inferno* is demonstrably closer to folk horror than *The Descent*, although it too has not been considered as such. Its central plot maps onto that of *The Descent*, and while its actors have different motives, they too are enmeshed in the colonialist project. The film follows a multinational (although mostly American) group of student-activists who travel to the interior of Peru in order to stop a logging company from destroying the forest and threatening the livelihood of an indigenous tribe. After their plane crashes, several of group are captured by the tribe they were trying to save and held in a cage until it is their turn to be ritualistically slaughtered and eaten. Folklore scholar Jeffrey Tolbert, on his Horror Folkloresque Research Project Facebook page, provocatively asks why *The Green Inferno* is not considered folk horror when Ari Aster's *Midsommar*, considered an exemplary folk horror film, has a virtually identical plot (minus the cannibalism): 'Both films', he writes, 'involve university-affiliated Americans going to a remote place and interacting with markedly "other" cultures. Both focus on these distant groups' isolation and insularity, both juxtapose their violent traditions with modern Western life, and both suggest that these anti-modern groups have a unique relationship to their local landscapes'. One of the group's participants, Craig Payst, answered this question by making the point that while *Midsommar* depicts its community as 'folk', *The Green Inferno* depicts its tribe as wholly 'other'.[76]

This point about the distinction between 'folk' and the 'other' gets to the heart of a principal distinction between folk horror and horror: the Peruvian tribe that captures the main characters in *The Green Inferno* are rendered so profoundly and terrifyingly 'other' that nothing of what they do becomes

---

[74] Marriott, *Descent*, p. 48.
[75] *The Descent: Part 2* (2009) diverges from the first film in ways that extend the former's folk horror leanings, which I explore at greater length in Dawn Keetley, 'Sacrifice Zones in Appalachian Folk Horror', in Dawn Keetley and Ruth Heholt (eds.), *Folk Horror: New Global Pathways* (Cardiff: University of Wales Press, 2023), pp. 245–61.
[76] Horror Folkloresque Research Project, 17 December 2021, www.facebook.com/groups/horrorfolkloresque.

explicable as tradition or ritual to the main characters and thus, by extension, to the viewers. The natives' rituals are portrayed as sheer horrific violence: one of the American students has each of his limbs cut off while he is still alive, for instance. In response to the violence, the captives scream, sob, throw up, even commit suicide in their horror at this encounter; only one character, the survivor Justine (Lorenza Izzo), connects with one villager – a boy – on something that approximates a human level. In *Midsommar*, on the other hand, while there is, to be sure, a profound gulf between the Americans and the villagers, there are intermediaries who explicate the latter's rituals and who thus render them legible as 'folk', even when violence intrudes. Race and nationality are also clearly at play in demarcating the dark and unruly Peruvians, who swarm their captives in an inchoate group, from the white, 'clean', and orderly inhabitants of the Swedish village, who are often literally arrayed in neat lines (Figure 3). Exploiting racial difference, then, Roth depicts his native tribe as so profoundly and inexplicably alien that they are more akin to the monstrous, barely human crawlers of *The Descent* than the structured and recognisably human community of *Midsommar*. Carroll has pointed out that the horror genre exploits 'the repelling aspect of existing creatures' by '*massing* them'[77] – and the visually dehumanised native 'mass' of *The Green Inferno* is thus all the more cast as horror's uncategorisable and 'impure' monster, not folk horror's legible community.

Figure 3 The neat 'pure' rows in *Midsommar* and the 'massed' villagers in *The Green Inferno*

Source: *Midsommar*, directed by Ari Aster (Square Peg, 2019); *The Green Inferno*, directed by Eli Roth (Worldview Entertainment, 2013).

---

[77] Carroll, *Philosophy*, p. 50.

2.3 Midsommar

While tracking a very similar plot as *The Green Inferno*, Ari Aster's *Midsommar* has (unlike the former) been categorised as an exemplary folk horror film, clearly influenced by Robin Hardy's equally paradigmatic *The Wicker Man* (1973).[78] That influence centres attention especially on the way in which ritual and tradition in *Midsommar*, as in its predecessor, are an integral part not only of the plot but of the very landscape. The highly scripted acts of the villagers of *Midsommar* are, then, a far cry from the shocking and 'inexplicable' actions of *The Green Inferno*'s tribe. *Midsommar* follows four Americans – Josh (William Jackson Harper), Mark (Will Poulter), Christian (Jack Reynor) and Dani (Florence Pugh) – who are invited by their Swedish postgraduate friend (and cultural intermediary), Pelle (Vilhelm Blomgren), to visit his small community, the Hårga, during its nine-day midsummer celebration. Like *The Wicker Man*, *Midsommar* includes not only a culminating sacrificial fire but also a narrative strategy of planting 'clues' that foreshadow what will happen to its protagonists, indicating that their fate is predetermined. Director Robin Hardy has famously said that *The Wicker Man* is constructed as a kind of 'game', with 'the hunter leading the hunted'.[79] In *Midsommar*, similarly, the American students think they are doing one thing (in this case, pursuing data on rituals at the Swedish village), completely unaware that (like Howie in *The Wicker Man*) they have from the beginning been intended as sacrifices in those very rituals. Just as Hardy does, Aster plants clues in the mise-en-scène that the Americans have already been chosen as victims: objects, art works and even the land itself disclose the traditions that will determine their fate. Both plots are scripted from the beginning, destinies determined from the start, and the protagonists progress inexorably towards their endings.

Midsommar is exemplary folk horror in that its central antagonists – the Hårga – live by an elaborate set of rituals, rooted in tradition and inscribed in their art, their sacred texts, their buildings and their land. They follow tradition, but it is important to note that they are depicted as doing so consciously and willingly. Their choice is evident in the explicitness of their beliefs and practices, as they describe them to the Americans as well as express them in both their art and landscape (even the design and placement of their buildings

---

[78] Owen Gleiberman claims that *Midsommar* is a 'veritable remake' of *The Wicker Man*. Owen Gleiberman, '"Midsommar": Destined to Be Controversial', *Variety*, 4 July 2019, https://variety.com/2019/film/columns/midsommar-destined-to-be-controversial-ari-aster-florence-pugh-1203259778/ [last accessed 15 April 2023].

[79] Robin Hardy, 'The Genesis of *The Wicker Man*', in Benjamin Franks, Jonathan Murray and Stephen Harper (eds.), *The Quest for The Wicker Man: History, Folklore, and Pagan Perspectives* (Edinburgh: Luath, 2006), p. 19.

articulate their traditions). The 'horror' in this exemplary folk horror emerges slowly, as the inherent and quite intentional violence of the Hårga's traditions are gradually revealed to the Americans, not least in the 'Ättestupa' ritual, in which two villagers who have reached the age of seventy-two jump from a cliff. Their non-coerced leap makes their volition evident. These scenes shock the visiting Americans and edge the film into a folk *horror* terrain where it will remain through the murder of most of their group and the culminating burning-alive of Christian encased in a bear skin. In the end, the Hårga are inherently violent, their community predicated on intentional ritual murder, and they are thus cast as monstrous.

2.4 The Ritual

Released two years before *Midsommar*, David Bruckner's *The Ritual* was also labelled an exemplary folk horror film by reviewers, many of whom welcomed it as part of the 2010s folk horror resurgence.[80] *The Ritual* is, though, also Folk Gothic, and it is a particularly useful text through which to explore the moment when folk horror becomes Folk Gothic. *The Ritual* shares the typical plot of folk horror: a group of friends explicitly delineated as modern, urban and cosmopolitan travel to a rural location and encounter an isolated and 'primitive' community. *The Ritual* begins in a city pub as five old friends – Luke (Rafe Spall), Dom (Sam Troughton), Hutch (Robert James-Collier), Phil (Arsher Ali) and Robert (Paul Reid) – plan their next 'lads' outing. The world is clearly their playground, and they debate the pros and cons of going to Ibiza, Amsterdam, Tuscany, Berlin and Belgium. (Later in the film, they take a group selfie, all saying 'Brexit', clearly ridiculing the provincialism they associate with those in Britain who voted to take their country out of the European Union.) Later that evening, as the rest of the group insists on going home at a reasonable hour, Luke drags Robert with him into a liquor store; inside, Robert stumbles on a burglary and is stabbed to death while Luke hides and watches. The film then cuts from Luke staring in horror at Robert's body pooled in blood to a close-up of his face, his eyes opening. It is six months later, in northern Sweden, and the four remaining friends, in honour of their dead friend, have come to hike the King's Trail, which runs between Sweden and Norway; hiking this trail had been Robert's proposal for their next outing, a suggestion they had mocked just before his death. As the friends travel further into the forest, they slowly realise that they are being hunted by the monstrous Jötunn, the bastard son of Loki,

---

[80] See, for instance, Tara Brady, 'The Ritual: The Folk Horror Revival Continues, So Stay out of the Woods', *The Irish Times*, 10 October 2017, www.irishtimes.com/culture/film/the-ritual-the-folk-horror-revival-continues-so-stay-out-of-the-woods-1.3249825 [last accessed 25 March 2023].

from Norse mythology – a deity worshipped by the inhabitants of a small isolated community living deep in the woods.[81]

On the one hand, *The Ritual* is indisputably folk horror in the clear, structuring border it establishes between the urban and the rural, the global and the rooted; it also features an unambiguous 'monster' (the Jötunn), bodily violence and gore, as well as forward, linear movement through space. As Luke says at one point, 'We're going to keep on walking until we get out of this fucking forest'. However, the important early cut from the English city to the close-up of Luke in a tent on the Swedish mountain signals the film's movement into Folk Gothic terrain. It crucially replaces the expected folk horror scene of the four friends actually traveling to Sweden, the long shots of vehicles traversing borders (on display in *The Descent*, *The Green Inferno*, and *Midsommar*). The usual linearity of folk horror is, in other words, interrupted by this cut. The cut signals, instead, a shift towards the entrapping and recursive temporal and spatial relations of the Gothic.

Indeed, the rest of the film unspools as, among other things, Luke's inner journey, as he continues to wrestle with the trauma of Robert's death and his guilt over doing nothing to help him. The film shifts into the Gothic register, in short, because Luke ventures into the forest and discovers that *he* – what he has sought to repress and disavow about himself – is the 'monster'. *The Ritual* is thus in the tradition of Gothic texts such as Nathaniel Hawthorne's 'Young Goodman Brown' (1835), in which the protagonist runs through the forest in terror at external monsters (witches, savage Indians, even the Devil himself) while the narrator declares that, in truth, 'all through the haunted forest, there could be nothing more frightful than the figure of Goodman Brown' himself.[82] *The Ritual* marks this lingering in Gothic terrain primarily through a scene that repeats four times: each time, Luke wakes up in the forest only to find himself back in the liquor store with his dying friend; each time, the liquor store becomes slightly more overwhelmed by the forest, indicating that Luke is grappling with the psychological effects of what happened there as well as what is happening in the woods. When Luke finally escapes the forest and turns from beyond its boundary line and screams at the creature that has killed all his friends, it is a form of catharsis: he has confronted his fears, his guilt and inadequacy, and conquered them. He has successfully transferred his feeling of responsibility for Robert's death (along with the deaths of his other friends) to

---

[81] Jack Wilhelmi, 'The Ritual's Creature Jötunn and Norse Mythology Origins Explained', *ScreenRant*, 18 November 2021, https://screenrant.com/ritual-movie-creature-jotunn-origin-norse-mythology-explained/ [last accessed 22 January 2022].

[82] Nathaniel Hawthorne, 'Young Goodman Brown' (1935), in *Nathaniel Hawthorne: Tales and Sketches* (New York: Library of America, 1996), pp. 276–89 (p. 284).

the 'monster' which he alone has overcome – and the film thus, with its drawing of a clear border between Luke and the monster, returns to folk horror.

Both the horror plot of *The Ritual* (with its very real, external 'monster') and the more or less traditional Gothic plot – confronting *individual* sins – is also interwoven with a specifically *Folk* Gothic narrative: the film is driven, after all, by the central ritual of the film's title. At first, it seems that the title refers to the ritual enacted in the second scene, once Luke, Dom, Phil and Hutch are in Sweden, when they memorialise their dead friend around a stone cairn on the windswept mountainside. Soon, though, it becomes clear that another ritual, not the one the friends planned, structures the film – and they have no control over this ritual; instead, it is marked into the landscape, and it controls them. After Dom injures his leg, the friends decide to abandon the hiking trail and take a shortcut through the forest that lies in the valley between them and the lodge. They soon become lost, disoriented, and, when a storm sweeps through, they end up spending the night in an abandoned house swallowed within the forest, surrounded by trees scratched with strange symbols and replete with a mysterious effigy on the second floor (Figure 4). They all have very bad dreams that night, dreams that turn out to foretell what is about to happen: Hutch is so terrified by what he dreams that he urinates on himself and refuses to discuss it; Phil wakes up to find he has walked upstairs, stripped off his clothes and is praying in front of the effigy; Luke has patterned wounds on his chest.

The next day, first Hutch and then Phil are killed by the creature that inhabits the woods. Dom and Luke discover their particular fates in the small community they discover still deeper in the forest, a community structured around the

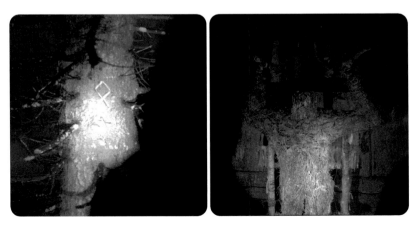

Figure 4 The ritualistic markings on the tree and the strange figure in the hut
Source: *The Ritual*, directed by David Bruckner (The Imaginarium, 2017).

worship of that creature: Dom is to be sacrificed, but Luke is to join the community, a fate foretold by the marks etched on his chest. Luke asks the young woman who brings him food, 'What is it?' She tells him, 'A god. Ancient. One of the Jötunn. A bastard offspring of Loki. We do not say its name'. She adds that worship of the god lets the villagers 'live beyond natural life' and that Luke's ritual will begin that night: 'You will kneel before the god'. Her words articulate Luke's fate as an inevitability ('you will'): he was chosen the first night the friends entered the forest. While his friends were killed and hung in the trees as sacrifices, he 'will kneel before it, like the rest of us', the woman tells him. The moment the group entered the forest, the moment they diverged from the public path they had mapped for themselves, they descended into a forest terrain in which their path was chosen for them, marked out on trees, artefacts, buildings and their own bodies.

   In a moment that indicates the friends are already trapped in a ritual, even before they appear to be, even before they know they are, even when they seem to still be pursuing their own ritual of memorialising Robert, they pass a Volkswagen bus abandoned on the mountain and one of them mutters, 'Everything in this bastard country's a relic'. As well as expressing the central conflict of the film – between the friends' commitment to a modern mobility and the 'ancient' world they are about to enter, centred on the 'relic' – this line also foreshadows their fate: they will encounter a 'relic', the 'bastard offspring of Loki', that is itself worshipped by 'relics', adherents whose lives the Jötunn has extended; and this 'primitive' cult is a 'relic' in contemporary Sweden. They do not know it yet, but the friends' lives are now determined by the 'ancient' beliefs and practices of a land they only knew how to exploit for their own pleasure. The 'primitive' beliefs that they believed were thoroughly surmounted, that they believed were quaint curiosities to be raised in facile conversation (Hutch earlier remarked glibly that the mountains were 'smashed out by Nordic gods'), in fact persist; they are embodied in the 'relics', animate and inanimate, that they discover in the forest. The presence of the decaying bus, moreover, along with the buried camping equipment they find from hikers who passed here before them, shows that they are not alone: the ritual and its god take all those who try to pass through, bending them to the same reiterated rituals. The symbols on the trees, the effigy, the god and its cult take over, dooming those who encounter them to the same predetermined fate.

   The Ritual is certainly in horror terrain with its central 'monster', the Jötunn, and it hovers on the edges of folk horror in that it depicts the encounter of a cosmopolitan group with a quite human community – as in *Midsommar* (and *The Wicker Man* before it). This encounter is not quite what it seems, though, and is importantly different from the superficially similar plot of *Midsommar*.

The community of worshippers in *The Ritual*, unlike the villagers in *Midsommar*, are disclosed to have little if any control over their rituals. Like Luke, Dom, Phil and Hutch, they are drawn into a ritual that is shaped by their 'god'. It is the Jötunn that decides whom it will sacrifice and who will be compelled to worship it. And the will of the Jötunn, which remains unnamed ('We do not say its name'), is dispersed throughout the forest, immanent in the trees it marks and on which it hangs its similarly marked victims. The 'community' of the film is, in the end, barely such; it is composed mostly of rotting 'relics' that straddle the line between animate and inanimate. And when the only person who speaks at all tells Luke what is happening, she emphasises the power of the 'it', of something other than human will: 'It keeps us here, lets us live beyond natural life'. She tells Luke that he has no choice: 'You will kneel before it, like the rest of us'. In the end, then, *The Ritual* offers a drama that is far from the very human dramas shaped in *The Wicker Man* and *Midsommar*: it is Folk Gothic precisely to the extent that it displaces the human world in order to illuminate the power of the non-human.

Early in the film, Robert tells his friends that the 'King's Trail' is like the Appalachian Trail but 'there's more history than hillbillies'. And it is larger impersonal processes, more like 'history' than 'hillbillies', that grip the friends once they enter the forest. 'The ritual' of the film's title names a recursive pattern, rooted in inexorable 'history' and 'tradition' and merged with the forest itself and the non-human 'relics' within it. Indeed, the titular 'ritual' conforms to what Barry Stephenson has argued is the definitive characteristic of ritual: *it* serves as 'an actor in its own right'; *it* has 'force, power, efficacy, or agency'.[83] The ritual seizes those who enter its uncanny space, forcing them – if they survive – to remain rooted in the forest, themselves eventually becoming barely animate, forged by the ritual into a 'relic' that is very much less than human.

2.5 Pet Sematary

Like *The Ritual*, Mary Lambert's 1989 adaptation of Stephen King's *Pet Sematary* (1983) is a hybrid of folk horror and Folk Gothic, exemplifying the points of intersection and divergence. Despite not making an appearance in Adam Scovell's otherwise comprehensive 2017 monograph, *Pet Sematary*'s inclusion in the folk horror canon is recognised in Kier-La Janisse's documentary, *Woodlands Dark and Days Bewitched: A History of Folk Horror* (2021), which features the film in its discussion of American folk horror's dependence on the 'Indian Burial Ground' trope. *Pet Sematary*'s narrative structure certainly positions it within folk horror, as the film begins with a young family moving

---

[83] Stephenson, *Ritual,* pp. 70–1.

from Chicago to Ludlow, Maine, where they soon learn the 'old ways' of the rural community. Immediately after arriving, they meet their neighbour Jud Crandall (Fred Gwynne), who has lived in Ludlow his entire life and who tells the Creeds the 'story' of the decades-old 'Pet Sematary' behind their house and, later, initiates Louis Creed (Dale Midkiff) into the power of the former Micmac tribal land 'beyond the barrier', land that returns any dead who are buried there. Jud tells Louis the lore of this land, just as he himself was told, decades ago, by a 'ragman', who was 'half Micmac himself'.

Pet Sematary's grounding in the modern world's encroaching on a rural town still characterised by the 'old ways' (white and Indigenous), is evident not only in the migration of the Creed family but in the fact that a small road that runs right by the Creeds' property has become a highway for trucks, linking rural Maine with the rest of the country. In King's novel, Jud tells Louis that most of the trucks are from Orinco, a chemical fertilizer factory, but there are also 'oil tankers, and the dump trucks, and the people who work in Bangor or Brewer' – all serving to destroy the 'peace' of the town.[84] The destructiveness of this burgeoning economic development, extending into formerly isolated regions of rural America, is most evident, of course, in the fact that university student Victor Pascow, the Creeds' cat Church and then the young Gage Creed himself will all be hit and killed by these trucks.

Lambert's *Pet Sematary* emphasises the mobility and displacement essential to folk horror by including, near the beginning of the film, a scene of the Creed family driving up to their new house – and then, shortly after that, Ellie Creed yells to her parents, 'I see a path.' Indeed, repeated shots of roads, paths and barriers signal both movement and boundary-crossing. In her book on *Pet Sematary*, Shellie McMurdo has aptly claimed that Lambert's film is 'predicated on boundaries'.[85] As well as the road itself, which embodies the modern encroaching into the rural, Lambert's camera also frequently tracks down the path that leads into the woods behind the Creeds' home and then to the 'barrier' separating the home from the former Micmac burial ground beyond, the barrier that 'was not meant to be crossed'. These multiple border crossings – sites of multiple displacements – mark the fact that when white Americans travel from cities to rural spaces, making the journey that is so often, in folk horror, back to the 'old ways' of rural *white* folk, they are also encroaching on prior Indigenous land, tribes and traditions. Jud Crandall will introduce Louis Creed to both, to the traditions of post-war, white settler Ludlow – the village 'pet sematary' – as

---

[84] Stephen King, *Pet Sematary* (1983; New York: Gallery Books, 2018), p. 14.

[85] Shellie McMurdo, *Pet Sematary* (Liverpool: Auteur, 2023), p. 40.

well as to his own disastrous burial of his beloved dog in the Micmac ground beyond the barrier and to the traditions of those prior Indigenous inhabitants.

While *Pet Sematary* is folk horror in its insistent visual imagery of roads (mobility) and barriers (transgression), and in its central modern, urban family's movement into layered white settler and Indigenous spaces and burial practices, it is finally, I propose, Folk Gothic in the power it gives to the non-human, to a land whose power demonstrably precedes the stories, the folktales, told about it and that try to explain it. The repeated sentence – 'the barrier was not meant to be crossed' – gives grammatical subjectivity to the barrier. And when Jud explains to Louis about the land beyond, he explicitly attributes agency to it: 'Whatever lives in the ground, beyond the pet cemetery, ain't human at all.' He continues that the 'Indians knew that. They stopped using that burial ground when the land went sour . . . The place is evil.' Later, Jud says that 'the place might have made Gage die' after Jud introduced Louis to the place, incited its power by taking Louis there to bury Church. In short, in everything Jud says about the land beyond the barrier, he acknowledges its prior power: the Micmacs left because they felt that power – and Jud and then Louis are drawn there because of that power. As McMurdo writes, 'we see throughout the film that the ground, and perhaps even the landscape of Maine itself, has an omniscient influential power over the Creeds, lending a fatalistic edge to the narrative'.[86] A seemingly throwaway moment in the film emphasises the agency of the non-human within the narrative: a brief clip of a TV news broadcast describes how whales are '*beaching themselves*' on the Maine coast, and 'scientists don't know why'. Like the whales, the land *acts* in Lambert's adaptation; this is not 'cursed Indian land'[87] – this is *cursed land*, with a power that precedes its white *and* its Indigenous occupants.

The fact that Mary Lambert's adaptation of *Pet Sematary* refuses to diffuse the force of the land itself – marking her film's lingering in Folk Gothic terrain – is evident in that there is no monster, unlike in *The Ritual,* where the Jötunn stalks the forest and claims at least some of its power. This absence is especially striking given that King himself associated the power of the land beyond the barrier with the Wendigo. Noting that every horror story 'needs some sort of monstrous Other', Kevin Corstorphine writes that King gives us the Wendigo, which is 'behind everything'.[88] Amplifying the (folk) horror of King's novel,

[86] McMurdo, *Pet Sematary*, p. 51.

[87] McMurdo, *Pet Sematary*, p. 53. McMurdo goes on to discuss the horror trope of the Indian burial ground in Lambert's *Pet Sematary* (see pp. 53–6); for King's novel, see also Gesa Mackenthun, 'Haunted Real Estate: The Occlusion of Colonial Dispossession and Signatures of Cultural Survival in U.S. Horror Fiction', *Amerikastudien/American Studies*, 43:1(1998): 93–108; and Kevin Corstorphine, '"Sour Ground": Stephen King's *Pet Sematary* and the Politics of Territory', *Irish Journal of Gothic and Horror Studies*, 1 (2006): 84–98.

[88] Corstorphine, '"Sour Ground"', p. 89.

not least with the addition of children wearing animal masks processing to the pet cemetery, Kevin Kölsch and Dennis Widmyer's 2019 *Pet Sematary* also weaves the return of the dead with explicit folk tales of a Wendigo that lives in the former tribal lands beyond the barrier. As Jud (John Lithgow) tells Louis (Jason Clarke), the Wendigo is a 'myth passed down by old tribes'. And while it may be a 'crazy folk tale', Jud adds that 'there is something up there that brings things back'. Kölsch and Widmyer's film thus gestures to the presence of a 'monster', but, even in this adaptation, the place is paramount and the folktale about the Wendigo ends up seeming rather gratuitous. Jud tells Louis about the Wendigo and shows him a picture in a book, but (again, unlike the Jötunn in *The Ritual*), it never materialises (just as the Wendigo never explicitly appears in King's novel). But even with the addition of what are, by 2019, the conventional cinematic tropes of folk horror as well as the 'monster' of horror, Kölsch and Widmyer's film still follows Lambert's in emphasising what Jud calls 'the power of that place'.

In an essay on the trope of the Indian burial ground and colonial dispossession, Gesa Mackenthun argues that King's novel attributes the power of the cursed land to the Micmac tribe, promoting the idea that 'the evil powers of the place derive from the land *and were fueled by ancient Indian rituals*', adding that the novel translates 'the horrors of colonial dispossession into a horror emanating from the country *and its inhabitants*'.[89] This argument foregrounds the human – the tribe. Importantly, though, in Lambert's adaptation, the Micmac people and the white settlers alike meet the eerie recalcitrance of the land itself. As Jud tells Louis, the Micmacs 'stopped using that burial ground when the ground went sour' – and they left. 'The place is evil', he concludes. *It's the land that acts* here, dictating both white settler and Indigenous traditions and movements.

2.6 In the Earth

While *The Ritual* and *Pet Sematary* are both hybrids of folk horror and Folk Gothic, I propose that Ben Wheatley's 2021 film *In the Earth* stands as an exemplary Folk Gothic film. Crucially (like *The Ritual* and *Pet Sematary*), it centres a ritual that has been repeatedly enacted in a specific landscape – in this case near a lone standing stone in a broad swathe of isolated English woodlands. This ritual has been given meaning by the folklore surrounding the mysterious figure of Parnag Fegg. To a much greater degree than *The Ritual* and even *Pet Sematary*, however, *In the Earth* posits the primacy of the non-human in its representation of its reiterated ritual: its ritual is not driven at all by humans but

---

[89] Mackenthun, 'Haunted Real Estate', pp. 101–2; emphasis added.

by the stone, the trees, the mushrooms and the vast network of mycorrhiza that lies under the forest – perhaps even the entire nation. And whereas the Jötunn in *The Ritual* and even the Wendigo in *Pet Sematary* are embodied as identifiable 'monsters' (even if the Wendigo only appears in the 2019 adaptation, and in the pages of a book), the folkloric figure of Parnag Fegg is never embodied, instead figuring the varied ways in which humans try to explain what is actually the efficacy of the natural world. *In the Earth* thus exemplifies the Folk Gothic, I argue, because it peels away human folklore – the stories we tell, the patterns we seek – and discloses their rootedness in the non-human. It is for this reason that the ritual (and thus the narrative itself) is recursive, bound as it is to the underlying 'cause' of nature itself. Humans are mere epiphenomena, not themselves the prime cause. Not coincidentally, then, the visual aesthetics of the film foregrounds the natural world and the objects within and associated with it, offering a plenitude of extreme long shots and close-ups. Both the narrative and mise-en-scène, in other words, make clear the Folk Gothic's stake in ecological critique.

In the Earth begins as Dr Martin Lowery (Joel Fry) arrives at Gantalow Lodge research site. He has lost communication with Dr Olivia Wendle (Hayley Squires) and is planning to hike into the forest to find her. Alma (Ellora Torchia) has agreed to guide him. Both Martin and Olivia are (ostensibly) involved in a research project studying crop growth, exploring specifically how plant roots create a 'mycorrhizal mat' in the fertile soil of the woods (a symbiotic interweaving of plant and fungus). On the second day of their hike, Martin and Alma are attacked and held prisoner by Zach (Reece Shearsmith), who dresses them in strange costumes, marks their bodies and drugs them so he can take staged photographs of them. Martin and Alma finally escape, stumbling onto Dr Wendle's camp and learning that she believes she has discovered how to communicate with the trees.

Before he and Alma set off into the forest, Martin sees a reproduction of a large woodcut on the wall of the lodge. Alma tells him it depicts Parnag Fegg, a 'local folktale', and she adds that 'She's a spirit of the woods'.[90] The woodcut reappears later, when Martin and Alma are captured by Zach, and Zach tells a different and more elaborate story about it. In his version, Parnag Fegg was a necromancer who was persecuted and chased into the forest. When his persecutors entered the woods in pursuit of him, however, all they found was an ancient standing stone, into which the necromancer's spirit had gone,

---

90 Ben Wheatley was asked about the inspiration for the local folk tale of 'Parnag Fegg' in the Q&A after *In the Earth*'s premiere at Sundance, and he replied that it was 'made up from scratch' and that it was 'non-sense' – perhaps explaining the trajectory of the film from folklore to science (and perfectly illustrating the 'folkloresque').

'transferred into the ancient matter of the forest', Zach says. Zach claims to talk to 'Him' and seems intent on sacrificing Martin and Alma to him: 'He has sent me so many people', Zach tells them, ominously. Olivia Wendle tells a third and still different story of Parnag Fegg, one that likewise centres on the ancient standing stone. She believes, however, that what is being channelled through the stone is not a long-dead necromancer but nature itself – the 'noise of the trees' and the vast web of mycorrhiza that lies under and connects the trees.[91] Like Zach, Olivia is also driven to offer sacrifice, but not to appease a deity, an all-powerful 'Him'. She believes that ritual sacrifice near the stone will amplify the voice of the trees, make it audible, comprehensible, to her. As she tells Martin, 'It all emanates from the standing stone. This is where there is the densest cluster of mycorrhiza. It regulates the forest for about thirty square miles, but I think it could be bigger still . . .. Nature is one giant system. This is the key to communicate with it'. Despite Olivia's express orientation towards the natural world, her beliefs are still articulated through folklore, however, through Parnag Fegg, the stone and an ancient copy of the fifteenth-century witch-hunting treatise, *Malleus Maleficarum*, which she claims has sections inserted into it about Parnag Fegg that guide her efforts to communicate with the trees. The different and yet overlapping stories about Parnag Fegg told by Alma, Zach and Olivia demonstrate how folklore emerges as a way to grasp the mysteries of the natural world. Both Zach and Olivia enjoin a ritual – sacrifice by a standing stone – in order to tap into, to try to understand, the powerful and determinative forces of the natural world around them.

The non-human world is indeed determinative in *In the Earth*, even more than in *The Ritual* (in which the characters at least appear to, or think they, choose their path). In a critical scene, Olivia tells Martin that, when she was drawn to that location, to the stone in the woods above the web of mycorrhiza, it 'was like I didn't have a choice'. Indeed, she couldn't purposefully seek out the stone because it simply 'doesn't appear on any maps'. Instead, it drew her to it. Then Zach showed up because he, too, 'couldn't deny the urge'. Olivia asks Martin about his motivation in coming: 'The thought, did it grow inside you like a seed . . . A voice in your head you couldn't deny?', and his silence offers his assent. All three of them, moreover, suffered from ringworm, and this fungal infection, tellingly manifest as circles on the skin, brought all three into a reiterated drama that has been going on indefinitely. Olivia speculates to

---

[91] In the Q&A after *In the Earth*'s premiere at Sundance, Wheatley claimed that the film was influenced by 1970s British horror and sci-fi, and he specifically mentioned Nigel Kneale who, among many other productions that have been labelled folk horror, wrote 1972's *The Stone Tape* with its central conceit of stone as a medium of communication. Unlike *In the Earth*, however, the titular stone of *The Stone Tape* channels very human ghosts.

Martin, 'the mycorrhizal network, it draws resources to the forest from many miles and maybe it brought you too'. Her comment notably marks Martin (as well as herself and Zach) as 'resources' for the forest – fungible, massed, and distinctly *not* bounded individuals. The mycorrhiza brought all of them, 'pushing our bodies in certain directions'. Impressing itself in their thoughts, imprinted on their bodies in the circular mark of ringworm, the vast mycorrhizal network drew all three characters into the forest, enfolding them in its ritual, harnessing them (in Olivia's view) in order to articulate its own need to maintain its ecology intact – its food, its shelter.

The end of the film moves towards a kind of narrative disintegration – a failure to adhere to human narrative forms – that constitutes the sign, I argue, of a definitive shift from the familiar human-centred story to one that traces the non-human. Ben Wheatley has talked of how the sound design actually delivers the noise of the trees (just as Olivia is trying to do within the narrative). Visually, the film ends with a montage of flickering images, intercut moments in the characters' stories and the forest, trees and stone. There is a reiterated and central shot in the film, moreover, one that begins and ends it, of the forest through the hole in the standing stone – a shot that seeks precisely to deliver the perspective of the natural world (Figure 5). In each iteration of this shot, there is no human looking. The shots appear early in the film, for instance, before the viewer knows about the folklore in which locals have shrouded the stone. They also appear near the end, accompanied by a soundtrack that was partially created using plants. In both cases, the stone and the nature of which it is a part, the forest and the mycorrhiza, stand as sole actors. The non-human life 'speaks' and draws the characters to the forest.

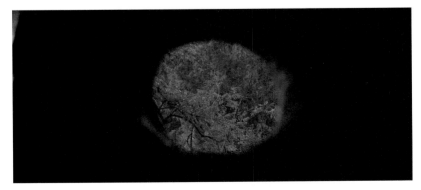

Figure 5 The shot – the impersonal look – through the stone's hole
Source: *In the Earth*, directed by Ben Wheatley (Rook Films, 2012).

In the Earth is Folk Gothic, then, in the way that it centres nature as an actor in the world, not merely a bit player in a human drama. Nature itself is the source of the folktales, the stories of Parnag Fegg, for instance, which are just attempts by the local community to explain the mystery of the woods. The forces beyond that impinge on human actors are rendered most literally in the web of fungi, which enmeshes the human characters. Kevin Trumpeter has written that, 'Although for reasons of legal convenience we like to identify discrete agents who can assume primary responsibility in any given situation, the reality is that events occur rather haphazardly as the result of a swarm of competing agencies. Causes are conventionally figured as chains (objects that are linear and therefore easy to trace from cause to effect), but webs or networks offer more apt metaphors'.[92] Adam Scovell has, of course, famously described folk horror through the metaphor of the chain, with its linked and human causality, what Jamie Chambers has called 'a four-part narrative teleology'.[93] With its central figure of a 'mycorrhizal mat' that underlies and determines everything, *In the Earth* embodies Folk Gothic as instead a web or mesh, one that entangles and subordinates human actors to its own distinct and non-human agency.

3 Folk Gothic Things

'Randalls Round', 'The Temple', 'The Flint Knife'

Objects – threatening objects – have long been an integral part of the Gothic. As Fred Botting put it in 1996, the Gothic inevitably includes 'the partial visibility of objects, in semi-darkness, through veils, or behind screens … denying a clearly visible and safe picture of the world'.[94] By 2019, Botting had shifted from describing Gothic objects seen only dimly in darkness to articulating the ways in which Gothic fictions 'are traversed' by 'darkly material disturbances, traces of unformed things operating beyond the reach of reason, rule and sense'.[95] In Botting's latest formulation, 'things' not objects are central to the

---

[92] Kevin Trumpeter, 'The Language of the Stones: The Agency of the Inanimate in Literary Naturalism and the New Materialism', *American Literature*, 87:2 (June 2015): 225–52 (p. 230).

[93] Scovell, *Folk* Horror, pp. 17–18. Scovell indicates a chain of causality – a 'horrific domino effect' – from one link in the chain to the next, from landscape to isolation to skewed beliefs to the culmination 'happening/summoning'. Chambers, 'Troubling Folk Horror', p. 10.

[94] Fred Botting, *Gothic* (New York: Routledge, 1996), p. 6.

[95] Fred Botting, 'Dark Materialism: Gothic Objects, Commodities and Things', in Jerrold E. Hogle and Robert Miles (eds.), *The Gothic and Theory: An Edinburgh Companion* (Edinburgh: Edinburgh University Press, 2019), pp. 240–59 (p. 240). Jeffrey Weinstock has a forthcoming book (of which I saw a manuscript draft of the first two chapters) that argues for the centrality of things to the Gothic: 'the Gothic has been insistently about objects and the material world as possessing what contemporary theorist Jane Bennett refers to as "thing-power"', and he proposes a reorienting of Gothic studies 'onto what might refer to as "Gothic materialism"'. Jeffrey Andrew

Gothic, and these 'things' are 'limit-figures' – 'registers of obscure destabilisation'.[96] Folklore has also been persistently about objects – about 'items', 'artefacts' and 'materials'.[97] As Dan Ben–Amos puts it, 'most definitions have conceived of folklore as a collection of things' and of 'material objects'.[98] These objects have, however, typically been subordinated to the individuals and communities who create, exchange and use them. Barre Toelken has argued that the folkloric object, such as a quilt or a barn, 'extends far beyond its *mere thingness* or its function'; instead, it 'expresses' particular 'personal' and 'cultural values'. Folkloric objects reflect 'the tastes of the local network of people for whom they perform'.[99] Even within Toelken's formulation, though, there are the seeds of a different notion of the 'vernacular materials' of folklore when he writes that, actually, they compose a 'tradition', or a 'compendium of those pre-existing culture-specific materials . . . that bear upon the performer more heavily than do his or her own personal tastes and talents'.[100] 'Tradition' has power, denoting a more 'impersonal' conception of folkloric materials, one in which they – not the individual or community – hold sway.

In the end, for Toelken, the 'mere' things of folklore, disarmed, dissipate into the community, producing the dynamic of folk horror with its central isolated village or 'tribe'. The Folk Gothic, on the other hand, exploits what is latent but eventually suppressed in Toelken's formulation: the power of 'vernacular materials' and folkloric 'things' to accrue a power of their own beyond the grasp of any individual or collective. It is, after all, these 'things' that often persist as their human creators, performers and users pass away. In exemplary Folk Gothic tales, Eleanor Scott's 'Randalls Round' (1929) and E. F. Benson's 'The Temple' (1924) and 'The Flint Knife' (1929), antiquarian protagonists wander into eerie landscapes in which exactly such Folk Gothic 'things' hold sway.

3.1 From Artefacts to Things

The typical folk horror plot is now quite familiar: a group of modern, urban 'outsiders' venture into an isolated, often rural, community ruled by 'archaic', pagan beliefs. The Folk Gothic plot is not so familiar, and I propose here that its

---

Weinstock, *Gothic Things: Dark Enchantment and Anthropocene Anxiety* (New York: Fordham University Press, 2023).

[96] Botting, 'Dark Materialism', p. 243.

[97] Barre Toelken, *The Dynamics of Folklore* (Logan, UT: Utah State University Press, 1996), pp. 33–4.

[98] Dan Ben-Amos, 'Toward a Definition of Folklore in Context', in Américo Paredes and Richard Bauman (eds.), *Toward New Perspectives in Folklore* (Bloomington, IN: Trickster Press, 2000), p. 10.

[99] Toelken, *Dynamics*, p. 34; emphasis added.   [100] Toelken, *Dynamics*, p. 37

most characteristic form involves characters running up against the intransigence of an artefact – what eventually emerges as a non-human 'thing' that stops them in their tracks, divesting them of agency and defying their way of knowing the world. The power of this artefact is not entirely unknown, as it is already an object of lore: those who have lived near it have shrouded it in stories, attempted to mitigate its uncanny power by weaving tales that tame it. My use of two terms here – artefacts and things – is important: the first marks the human effort to make artefacts of things and the second marks the tendency of things to dodge that effort, to escape their provenance as artefacts, to shake off their artefact-ness. An artefact is an 'object made or modified by human workmanship, as opposed to one formed by natural processes' – and, in archaeological terms, it is an 'excavated object that shows characteristic signs of human workmanship or use'.[101] Artefacts show evidence of human intervention, then, although that 'workmanship' is best characterised not as 'opposed' to 'natural processes' but as 'with' and 'through' nature. Artefacts are typically found or 'excavated' – hidden, at first, from 'modern' life but then discovered as profound interruptions to it, as they inevitably disclose their power as 'things'.

Jane Bennett has offered a thoroughgoing articulation of the ways that 'things' accrue power and act in the world: 'thing-power' is 'that which refuses to dissolve completely into the milieu of human knowledge'; it marks when the 'it' becomes 'an actant' and signals 'the moment of independence (from subjectivity) possessed by things'.[102] '*Thing-Power*', she continues, becomes manifest when objects acquire 'the curious ability . . . to animate, to act'.[103] Folk Gothic illuminates those uncanny and dread-inducing effects when 'things' materialise from 'artefacts' that have been unburied, excavated both from the earth and from the presumptions that they are wholly enshrined within human 'workmanship', within human history and knowledge. Folk Gothic is, indeed, above all driven by this emergence of artefacts as things, dramatising all of the paralysing and often violent effects of that emergence on the characters who unearth them.

Bound up with artefacts, Folk Gothic's compelling things are, moreover, also tied to particular places, ritual places, shaping a version of enclosed and entrapping Gothic space.[104] Folk Gothic things, specifically, inhabit places deemed sacred, although in the 'modern' time that forms the present of Folk Gothic narrative, these sacred places are typically cast as cursed. Alexandra Walsham has pointed out that when the Romans confronted the pagan beliefs of

---

[101] *Oxford English Dictionary*, 3rd ed. (Oxford: Oxford University Press, continually updated at www.oed.com/).
[102] Bennett, *Vibrant Matter*, p. 3.   [103] Bennett, *Vibrant Matter*, p. 6.
[104] See pp. 10–11 of this book.

those they tried to conquer, they called the places of pagan worship and ritual '*loci abhominati*'.[105] *Loci abhominati*, profane sites, were sites dedicated to deities other than Roman gods; they mixed nature with constructed objects – that is, they mixed woods, hills, trees, springs and caves with stone circles, barrows, wells, churches, knives and altars. Indeed, just as the human processes that crafted artefacts are not 'opposed' to natural processes, pre-modern people 'did not', Walsham points out, 'draw a rigid distinction between natural land-marks and the architectural structures that were an outgrowth of them'.[106] Part of the dread that infuses Folk Gothic, then, stems from the fact that its 'modern' protagonists encounter *loci abhominati* and the things that constitute them, first, with a sense that they are profane or even 'cursed', and, second, with a distinctly modern belief in the separateness of the (active) human and the (inert) non-human. That the *loci abhominati* and the things of the Folk Gothic profoundly challenge this view – that passive artefacts refuse to stay in their place and instead emerge as powerful things – is precisely part of the profaneness of those places and things: they are cursed and animate matter.

If Folk Gothic features a profane even cursed place that dissolves distinctions between human and thing and represents characters in thrall to both things and their places, it also disrupts time: time in the *loci abhominati* is not linear but iterative – Christopher Baldick's 'fearful sense of *inheritance in time*'.[107] One of the particular forms of the 'inheritance in time' of the Folk Gothic is manifest in ritual that is repeated through time, overwhelming any effort of characters to move forward, to move out or onward. In the Folk Gothic, ritual is constituted by non-human things; indeed, they are the drivers of rituals that demonstrably overcome the will of those who participate in them. Ritual, as Barry Stephenson has claimed, has 'force, power, efficacy, or agency' – and it is characterised by 'acts not constituted by the participant's intentions, but by prior stipulation and tradition'.[108] Folk Gothic distinctively embeds this autonomous agency of ritual in the agency of the things that constitute the ritual – the mask, the barrow, the altar, the knife, the stone. As modern protagonists encounter these things and the rituals they enact, moreover, they are wrenched from those familiar temporal and spatial frameworks that grant agency only to humans, that are tied to a structuring binary of passive non-human matter and agential humans. As Stephenson continues, 'in participating, the ritual actor relinquishes agency; one is no longer the author of one's own acts but conforms to the form and elements that comprise the rite'.[109] In Folk Gothic, characters no longer tell

---

[105] Alexandra Walsham, *The Reformation of the Landscape: Religion, Identity, and Memory in Early Modern Britain and Ireland* (New York: Oxford University Press, 2011), p. 24.
[106] Walsham, *Reformation*, p. 5.   [107] Baldick, 'Introduction', p. xix; emphasis added.
[108] Stephenson, *Ritual*, pp. 70–1, 83.   [109] Stephenson, *Ritual*, pp. 83–4.

their own stories in legible time and space but are drawn into the stories of things in static, sacred places and recursive, ritual time.

Because the things of Folk Gothic are (unearthed) artefacts before they are things, cognitive archaeology, in particular, serves as a useful lens through which to read them. Cognitive archaeology strives to understand the history (even prehistory) of the human mind through 'the material remains of the past'.[110] Cognitive archaeologist Lambros Malafouris has articulated what he calls 'Material Engagement Theory', which brings 'materiality – that is, the world of things, artefacts, objects, materials, and material signs – firmly into the cognitive fold', mapping a 'cognitive landscape in which brains, bodies, and things play equal roles in the drama of human cognitive becoming'.[111] According to Malafouris, material culture is not just passive 'evidence' or the 'external products'[112] of human minds; material culture always actively constitutes mind. Malafouris's Material Engagement Theory thus aims to dismantle what Bruno Latour has called the 'purification project of modernity', which 'habituated our minds to think and talk in terms of clean divisions and fixed categories', to conceptualise 'the isolated internal mind and the demarcated external material world'. We should instead, Malafouris claims, think of 'their mutual constitution as an inseparable analytic unit'.[113] Malafouris himself posits a 'gray zone of material engagement' – the *zone in which brains, bodies, and things conflate, mutually catalyzing and constituting one another*'.[114] The Folk Gothic, I argue, is a fictional enactment of material engagement, taking place precisely in this 'gray zone', a liminal space of entanglement of human and non-human actors.

Indeed, like Material Engagement Theory, the Folk Gothic profoundly challenges the 'purification project of modernity', a project the protagonists of Folk Gothic are all determined to undertake. It is not an accident that they are often scholars, antiquarians and archaeologists, all intent on fixing the external world of objects and artefacts *as* external. As the narrative moves, however, Folk Gothic inevitably demonstrates that 'brains, bodies, and things' are, as Malafouris describes, 'mutually catalyzing and constituting'. More than that, in fact. The Folk Gothic forges far beyond mutuality (which has never been an especially Gothic theme), dramatising instead how 'things' *overcome* bodies and brains. The scholars and antiquarians of Folk Gothic – conglomerates of human brains and bodies – strive to subjugate things as 'artefacts', and when things inevitably resist their subjugation, it looks a lot like an act of vengeance.

---

[110] Lambros Malafouris, *How Things Shape the Mind: A Theory of Material Engagement* (Cambridge, MA: The MIT Press, 2013), p. 1.
[111] Malafouris, *How Things*, p. 2.   [112] Malafouris, *How Things*, p. 3.
[113] Malafouris, *How Things*, p. 16.   [114] Malafouris, *How Things*, p. 5; emphasis in original.

While Folk Gothic 'things' profoundly challenge the world view of the 'modern' and 'rational' characters, moreover, the narrative also makes it clear that things have actually always retained their power within the domain of folklore: folklore has persisted in recognising the sacred sites and ongoing rituals that mark the power of things, striving to contain that power, to be sure, but much more loosely.

3.2 'Horrible, Primitive' Ritual in 'Randalls Round'

Eleanor Scott centres 'Randalls Round' on educated men, removed in every kind of way from the local and rural ritual that will ultimately undo one of them. As the story begins, Mortlake and Heyling are ensconced in Oxford, discussing with appropriate scholarly condescension traditional 'revivals' – what protagonist Heyling calls 'this folk-song and dance business'.[115] Since Heyling has been studying too hard, he has been advised by his tutor to take a break during the Michaelmas term and plans to take a holiday in the Cotswolds; Mortlake, clearly some sort of student of antiquarianism, asks Heyling if he can look up records in the guildhall of the village he's visiting, since it 'is believed to be one of the places where there is a genuine survival', a game or a dance 'called Randalls Round' (p. 22). Like M. R. James's curious antiquarians, who themselves unearth powerful artefacts,[116] an intrigued Heyling gets on his bicycle and heads into the 'wilds', where the landscape becomes 'more open, bleaker' (p. 22), eventually arriving at the small village of Randalls and checking in to his room at the Flaming Hand Inn (p. 23). Later that evening, Heyling's peace is disturbed by the sounds of chanting. Looking out of his window, he witnesses a ritual dance taking place on the village green. As it draws to its conclusion, a figure wearing a bull mask leads another figure shrouded in white into the middle of the green, where a pole supporting a 'shaggy hide' stands (p. 25). The dance culminates in the masked figure shaking this 'shaggy hide' from the top of a pole, so that it envelops the shrouded figure.

Heyling will later witness a second and terrifying enactment of the ritual, but after he watches the first dance on the green, he is able to assimilate the strange event into his rationalising worldview. The language of recognition pervades the early part of the story, which emphasises an antiquarian perspective seeking to confine the self-evidently 'archaic' to the past and subordinate objects to an anthropocentric perspective. Three times, as Heyling watches the villagers

---

[115] Eleanor Scott, 'Randalls Round', in Aaron Worth (ed.), *Randalls Round: Nine Nightmares* (London: The British Library, 2021), pp. 21–37 (p. 21). Further references to this story will be inserted parenthetically in the text.

[116] See M. R. James's stories 'Oh, Whistle, and I'll Come to You, My Lad' (1904) and 'A Warning to the Curious' (1925).

dance on the green, for instance, he is described as 'recognising' features of the ritual; he recognises the authenticity of the song, as well as some of the features of the dance (having 'seen folk-dancing done in Oxford'), and he even recognises the 'figure' the dancers form – the 'Back Ring' (pp. 24–5). As the dance continues, however, elements intrude that escape Heyling's 'faint stirrings of memory' (p. 25), specifically, artefacts that obscure the human participants: a 'mask made in the rough likeness of a bull' covering one figure's face; a white sheet shrouding another figure; and a 'hide' that hangs on a central pole (p. 25). At the culmination of the dance on the village green, when the figure in the mask jerks the pole and the 'shaggy hide fell outspread on the shrouded figure standing before it', the dance briefly spirals away from Heyling's ability to understand it at all. Indeed, it seems to him that these 'things' – mask, pole, hide – come alive. The scene 'gave a horrid impression – as if the creature hanging limp on the pole had suddenly come to life, and with one swift, terrible movement had engulfed and devoured the helpless victim standing passively before it' (p. 25). The artefacts of the ritual become animate – 'suddenly come to life'. In this moment, it is the human that is rendered 'passive' while things, emerging from their status as artefact, act.

What happens in the ritual, as Heyling tries and fails to apprehend it, approximates Bennett's 'thing-power', when objects acquire the 'curious' ability to 'act'. She notes the uncanniness of this moment: 'things' emerge 'when the subject experiences the object as uncanny'.[117] Heyling certainly experiences uncanniness when the mask, the shroud, the pole and the hide *act* together as what Bennett calls an 'agentic assemblage', when agency becomes 'distributed across an ontologically heterogeneous field'.[118] Indeed, rituals are expressly a locale of distributed agency. As Stephenson writes, ritual 'allows us to broaden our notion of agency. Normally, we think of agency as being located in individuals, having to do with matters of will, intentionality, choice, desire. But there is a wider, *distributed agency* at work in ritual'.[119] An uncanny brew of suddenly alive and animate things intervenes in the dance that Heyling thinks he recognises and remembers, rendering him 'shocked' (p. 25). This 'shock' marks precisely the moment that anthropocentric reason fails and things emerge, agency dispersed across the landscape. In that moment, the dancers themselves, as well as Heyling, recede into the background as the conglomerate of things – mask, shroud, pole and hide – take over, bound in a ritual that surpasses the intentions even of those who participate in the dance, enacting a more impersonal efficacy.

---

[117] Bennett, *Vibrant Matter*, pp. 2, 6. [118] Bennett, *Vibrant Matter*, pp. 21, 23.
[119] Stephenson, *Ritual*, p. 85; emphasis added.

Heyling's dislodging from the foreground of his own story is relatively fleeting at this point, as he immediately resorts to books to put him back in control, to help him assimilate what he has witnessed. After the dance ends, he pulls out a 'volume of a very famous book on folk-lore' that Mortlake had given him, which serves to re-frame the disturbing ritual through accounts that were 'as careful and well authenticated as the facts in a scientific treatise' (p. 26). Heyling learns that the dance he witnessed is 'almost certainly sacrificial' and has long been linked with Randalls Bank, a nearby mound 'almost certainly formed by a long barrow of the Paleolithic age' and surrounded by a thicket that the 'villagers refuse to approach' (p. 26). The authoritative facticity of this book – and the comforting reiteration of the 'almost certainly' – gives Heyling a mastery that continues the next day as he goes to the guildhall and spends the day poring over documents that all serve to render the barrow explicable: he reads a book about 'Prehistoric Remains in the Cotswolds' and legal documents concerning the barrow and the field and accusations of 'devil worship' (p. 29). Heyling finds the histories 'appalling', but the documents consistently frame the barrow and its rites as occurring a long time ago (the story includes sections of documents in their original, archaic language) and in a community marked as 'remote' and involving beliefs held by indubitably 'superstitious' locals (pp. 28–9).

His mastery bolstered, Heyling sets out to investigate the barrow that night: 'He began to feel some of the enthusiasm of the explorer' (p. 31). Heyling never does excavate the barrow, however. He arrives at the field in the darkness to experience a horrifying reiteration of the dance in a much more disorienting setting: it is dark; the participants have blackened their faces, blending into the night, their distinctiveness blurred, depersonalised. This dizzying dissolving of subjectivity in the darkness sets the stage for the final dominance of 'things'; indeed, what Heyling experiences is precisely the vastly more animate nature of the 'things' of the ritual – the shroud, the mask, and then some 'horrible primitive creature' – than in its earlier iteration. At the culmination of the ritual, Heyling buries his head, unable to 'think, or move, or pray' and only listens, hearing 'crunching, tearing' and 'lapping' and a 'crashing, snapping noise' (p. 36). When the ritual is over, he can only see 'things', without the ability to interpret them, and he stumbles away 'blindly' (p. 37). If 'thing-power' is, as Bennett puts it, 'that which refuses to dissolve completely into the milieu of human knowledge',[120] Scott's story ends with things having mastered its protagonist, as Heyling is disarmed of any authority his books and knowledge gave him – indeed, of his ability to reason, to know, at all.

---

[120] Bennett, *Vibrant Matter*, p. 3.

3.3 Ritual Things in 'The Temple' and 'The Flint Knife'

E. F. Benson published stories both before and contemporaneous with Scott's 'Randalls Round' that similarly feature visitors to a rural area who experience an ancient and potentially deadly ritual: in both cases, the stories attenuate still further the domination – indeed the mere presence – of humans in that ritual, dramatising the driving power of the artefact alone. Both 'The Temple' and 'The Flint Knife' are set in an isolated region of Cornwall, where a pair of educated men come to stay for a holiday and end up encountering formerly sacred spaces – *loci abhominati* that are described as 'Druidical' places of sacrifice. In 'The Temple', an unnamed narrator and his friend Frank Ingleton find a 'stone of sacrifice' in their kitchen after they ascertain that the house they have rented stands in the middle of a 'Druidical temple'.[121] One of the two men is then eerily compelled to immolate himself on the stone with a flint knife that appears out of nowhere in their garden. In the very similar 'The Flint Knife', an unnamed narrator and his friend Harry Pershore find a 'square column of black granite', which they speculate is 'some Druidical piece', in a walled-up area of vegetation in Harry's garden. After they knock a doorway in the wall, Harry becomes unerringly drawn towards it.[122] He is found by his friend one night, kneeling at the altar with an indeterminate figure in black holding his head back and brandishing something in his other hand. The next day, they find a flint knife on top of the granite stone.

These stories exemplify the Folk Gothic because they not only attribute power to artefacts but they also represent that power as enacted in long-forgotten rituals – reiterated rituals that have slipped entirely from the provenance of humans *to the ritual things themselves*. The principal critic to have discussed Benson's stories, Ruth Heholt, takes them up as hybrids of folk horror, the weird, and the ghost tale – and she argues that, to the extent that they embody folk horror, it is 'the *people in the landscape* who provide the focus of the horror'.[123] Reading 'The Temple' and 'The Flint Knife' as Folk Gothic rather than folk horror, I argue that it is the *things in the landscape* that serve as the focus. More specifically, both stories depict rituals centred on stone – granite pillars, megaliths, standing stones

---

[121] Edward Frederic Benson, 'The Temple', in *Night Terrors: The Ghost Stories of E. F. Benson* (Ware: Wordsworth Editions, 2012), pp. 517–31 (pp. 524–5, 518). Further references to this story will be inserted parenthetically in the text.

[122] Edward Frederic Benson, 'The Flint Knife', in Mike Ashley (ed.), *The Outcast and Other Dark Tales by E. F. Benson* (London: The British Library, 2020), pp. 209–23 (p. 216). Further references to this story will be inserted parenthetically in the text.

[123] Ruth Heholt, 'Sunny Landscapes, Dark Visions: E. F. Benson's Weird Domestic Folk Horror', in Dawn Keetley and Ruth Heholt (eds.), *Folk Horror: New Global Pathways* (Cardiff: University of Wales Press, 2023), pp. 145–65 (p. 161); emphasis added.

and sacrificial stone – illuminating Jeffrey Jerome Cohen's claim that stone, in particular, 'offers a stumbling block to anthropocentrism'.[124]

In acting with increasing autonomy, the artefacts in Benson's stories produce a profound sense of the 'eerie' that is integral to Folk Gothic and the ways in which it imagines both ritual and artefacts. The eerie denotes a moment when expectations of either presence or absence – what should be there or what should not – are profoundly disrupted. As Mark Fisher has aptly put it, the eerie denotes either 'a *failure of absence*' or 'a *failure of presence*'. He elaborates that the eerie is created when 'there is something present where there should be nothing, or there is nothing present where there should be something'.[125] The 'things' of Benson's stories – the sacrificial stone, the altar, the flint knife – embody both forms of eerie, each of which disturbs familiar anthropocentric stories. Benson's things are present 'where there should be nothing': they just appear, without context; they are relics of ancient times suddenly found within modern England. Out of space and time, they are present in a place and time they should not be. They drive rituals, moreover, that highlight the absence of humans: they should be directed by humans, the community that enacts and is bound by the rituals at the centre of these stories. But this community is what Fisher calls that 'nothing present where there should be something'. There are no people – what should be present is not there, or is at best a shadowy presence described mostly as 'unseen'. Abandoned by humans, the rituals are continued by artefacts. As Fisher develops his definition of the eerie, he argues that it is inextricable from the question of agency, specifically 'the agency of the immaterial and the inanimate: the agency of minerals and landscapes'.[126] When inanimate things appear from nowhere, when they are embedded in and as landscape, when they are present when and where they should not be, and when they act in the absence of humans, agency devolves only to them. The eerie ushers in, then, a haunting sense of a non-human agency.

In both of Benson's stories, as in 'Randalls Round', the main characters are described (vaguely) as scholars. As such, they enter spaces they are at first confident they can 'know'. In 'The Temple', Frank Ingleton is 'a student of those remains of prehistoric civilisations which are found in such mysterious abundance in the ancient county' of Cornwall (p. 517), and the narrator is trying to write a book on some unspecified topic. In 'The Flint Knife', the narrator possesses 'archaeological knowledge', which Harry Pershore asks him to bring to bear on the mysterious granite column they find in the walled-in garden.

---

[124] Jeffrey Jerome Cohen, *Stone: An Ecology of the Inhuman* (Minneapolis, MN: University of Minnesota Press, 2015), p. 6.
[125] Mark Fisher, *The Weird and the Eerie* (London: Repeater Books, 2016), p. 61.
[126] Fisher, *Weird*, p. 11.

Indeed, the narrator remembers seeing something like it 'in some Museum of early British remains', and he knows enough to be convinced that the column was 'certainly not Roman' and 'looked far more like some Druidical piece' (p. 216). Like Frank Heyling's encounter with the barrow in Scott's story, the protagonists of Benson's stories enter terrain dotted with ancient monuments, armed, they think, with the ability to understand them. Indeed, the stories set up a contrast between these modern and 'expert' visitors to the 'ancient county' of Cornwall, who are defined by a knowledge that forges a clear distinction between the past and the present, and the locals whose 'superstitions' allow the past to live on in the present. In 'The Temple', while the ancient religions marked by the stones were 'reckoned as abomination' once Christianity arrived, Frank Ingleton notes that 'old superstitions linger' in these rural and isolated places, reminding the narrator of a witchcraft trial that took place in Penzance a year ago (p. 519). The two local women who serve as housekeepers for the narrator and Frank embody this 'local' predilection for superstition, as they both refuse to stay overnight in the house, walking back and forth from the local village of St Caradoc's each day, even in a drenching thunderstorm (p. 524).

The protagonists of Benson's stories end up, however, discovering that the places in which they find themselves defy the knowledge they possess: they are eerie places, *loci abhominati* – profane and unnatural places of pagan worship. As Frank explains of a nearby stone circle in 'The Temple', 'something clings to it, some curse, some abomination' (p. 518), and this sense of the unnatural only intensifies as they explore the half-buried stones of the temple and the nearby woods: the air becomes oppressive and the place 'seemed thick with unseen presences' (p. 520). Likewise, when the narrator and Harry Pershore in 'The Flint Knife' knock out a door in the walled garden and enter, the narrator remarks that 'there was something deadly and oppressive about this hot torpor; the air was stagnant' (p. 215). The palpable feeling of stagnation that pervades the places of these ancient monuments indicates an entrenched *stasis*: time moves differently – and possibly not at all – here.

The sense of 'abomination' that lingers in these places is certainly on one level about the 'pagan' religions that were once practiced there. On another level, however, it is about the fact that these 'pagan' practices expressly foregrounded the non-human – what Frank in 'The Temple' called the 'blind powers of nature' – and that these powers demanded the sacrifice of humans (p. 519). The worldview in Benson's 'oppressive' *loci abhominati* is one in which things – mixed things of nature and non-human things – accrue an autonomy that they do not appear to have in the spaces and time of modernity. What is 'queer' and 'uncanny' in these stories – words repeatedly used – is that the artefacts the characters find start to exert control once they are found. And although these artefacts bear evidence of having been made by (with) humans, and although they thus embody the 'natural' interwoven with the human, it is the 'natural' part that is emphasised in both stories – the *granite* sacrifice stone and altar, the *flint* knife; humans remain 'unseen' presences, subordinated to those 'blind powers of nature'. What might be human figures are glanced in the distance, a dark figure seen far away, out of the corner of the eye. The granite and the flint, however, are a solid, real and urgent presence.

Indeed, the absence of people in the 'pagan' rituals of Benson's stories is striking. In 'The Temple', Frank is driven to repeat the ancient ritual of human sacrifice on the granite 'sacrifice stone' that now lies in their kitchen – and he is driven to do so by no discernible human entity, by just the stone and the knife. That this is indeed a ritual that has been repeated across time becomes evident when the narrator discovers that the former owner of the house, who ostensibly committed suicide, was found on the stone with his throat cut, and, beside him, 'was a sharp, curiously shaped fragment of flint' (p. 528). The source of horror in this story is 'the power, whatever that was, which had driven him to kill himself on the stone of sacrifice' (p. 529). The nature of this 'power' is unclear, and the story ends with multiple references to people, drums and pipes that the narrator 'imagines', to 'presences unseen and multitudinous', to the fact that the narrator 'saw and heard nothing, 'no touch of invisible hands', only 'the unseen' (p. 530), 'no visible adversary' and 'intangible hosts' (p. 531). What the narrator remains blind to, even at the end, however, is that while what he *expects* to see (humans) remains intransigently 'unseen', what *is* seen, what *is* visible, what *is* tangible – and what appears to act – is the granite stone and the flint knife.

In 'The Temple', then, ancient people, those who presumably engaged in 'pagan' rites, are evoked only in their invisibility, and the protagonists are left alone with ritual artefacts that have become powerful and agentic things. In 'The Flint Knife', on the other hand, a 'dark figure' does loom into view at the end, seemingly serving as another human who interacts with the protagonists, who draws them in to the ritual act of sacrifice. But this always-obscure and undefined figure actually only serves to confuse the boundaries between human and non-human, as it is persistently described as indistinguishable from the granite column. The night after Harry tells the narrator about the strange walled garden on his grounds, the narrator has a dream in which 'a tall upright figure' in its centre seemed to draw him closer. He adds, 'I could not make out whether it was a man or some columnar block of stone', although 'whether stone or flesh and blood, it seemed to be waiting' (p. 214). While the figure's 'nature' seems to be revealed when it appears to raise its arm (p. 214), the confusion persists, and, on another night, when the narrator and Harry pursue a dark figure, they find it in the middle of the walled-in garden, where 'it was as if the altar was one with it' (p. 219). Harry interprets this encounter by insisting that what they had seen was 'real and material' and thus 'must have been a man' (p. 220) – as if there are no other possibilities, no other 'real and material' things. Harry continues that the mystery of the man's vanishing must be due to the fact that 'we were both staring at the altar' while the man escaped, but the very construction of his sentence makes it clear that he is refusing to see what was right in front of him: they were both, in fact, 'staring at the altar' – and there was no 'man'. Harry and the narrator may in fact only be seeing a black granite column, their anthropocentric presumptions conjuring up the human figure they assume should be present.

The narrator of 'The Flint Knife' espouses a theory that actually grants power (of a kind) to things. He believes that homes and gardens 'absorb' the 'thoughts and personalities of those who have inhabited them' (p. 209). He believes, as his friend repeats back to him later, that 'material objects can absorb and give out force they have derived from living folk' (p. 221). But things are *not* inert matter that 'absorb' a 'force' 'derived from living folk'. They have 'force' of their own. As such, 'The Temple' and 'The Flint Knife' inhabit the eerie realm of the Folk Gothic, a realm in which events are driven by recursive time and the agentic power of place, including the active power of all the non-human things that constitute *loci abhominati*. Humans are absent or, at best, so firmly associated with ritual things (as in the granite column) that it's impossible to tell where one ends and the other begins. The narrator of 'The Flint Knife' struggles to grasp this unfamiliar and deeply unsettling reality: 'A lump of stone like that altar was just a lump of stone. How could it possess properties and powers such as those which I was disposed to attribute to it?' (p. 221). How indeed? But, the story suggests that it does, as both stone and flint compel Harry Pershore to an act he never conceived of himself.

In holding that 'living folk' impressed themselves on 'material objects', and in this way granting objects the only kind of power they could conceive them as having, the protagonists of the 'The Flint Knife' espouse a world view that Malafouris expressly challenges (and seeks to replace) in his Material Engagement Theory. He argues that there is 'a deeply entrenched "I-centric" bias in philosophical thinking', one that argues that the mind is strictly 'a property or possession of the individual', that 'the temporality of mind is constrained and determined by the temporality of the individual' and that 'the location of mind is coextensive with the organismic boundaries of the individual'.[127] Benson's 'The Temple' and 'The Flint Knife' profoundly challenge this belief. They depict what Malafouris calls 'the extended mind', which

---

[127] Malafouris, *How Things*, pp. 80–1.

is actually more akin to a 'cognitive system' dispersed through the world around it. In this cognitive system, memory, for instance, 'transcends the biological limitation of the individual person and becomes available "out there" for other people to use, comment on, transform, or incorporate'.[128] The stone monoliths, sacrifice stone, granite altar, and flint knives in Benson's stories are inherent parts of a 'cognitive system', a 'new ecology of memory' that 'cannot be reduced to any of its constituent parts'.[129] Granite and flint cannot, in other words, be reduced to the residual effects of 'living folk'.

While Benson's stories certainly illuminate Malafouris's theory of 'the extended mind' – 'cognitive assemblies' of 'neural, bodily, social, material' components, all in dynamic interaction[130] – they push this theory further, into specifically Gothic territory. Malafouris argues, for instance, that 'memory' is not rooted into the organic (and thus eventually decomposed) human individual but that it is (to repeat) 'available "out there" for other people to use, comment on, transform, or incorporate'.[131] This formulation still gives priority, and too much power, to humans: 'other people' are the subjects and they are the ones using, commenting on, transforming and incorporating. Benson's protagonists do this at first, bringing their scholarly knowledge to bear on the stones they find in the landscape, for instance. They comment on the monoliths and sacrifice stones, purporting to know their uses. In 'The Flint Knife', Harry plans to 'incorporate' the black granite monolith into his 'flower garden' and put a sundial on top of it (p. 217). But the stone has other 'plans'. In fact, Benson's stories enact an inversion of the power relationship instantiated in the structure of Malfouris's sentence. From a different perspective (one that Malafouris helps us arrive at), *the stone* draws Harry and the narrator to *it*, lures them to knock down the wall, to unearth it. From its perspective, Harry and the narrator are inert matter, 'available "out there" for' *it* 'to use, comment on, transform, or incorporate' (p. 82). Humans become the malleable resources of the non-human.

4 Folk Gothic's Place

The Owl Service, The Feast

In the last section, 'things' emerged from their dismissal as merely passive 'artefacts' or 'vernacular materials' exchanged by humans[132] and accrued a power of their own, driving rituals and thus attenuating human efficacy. This section considers not only the role of things in Folk Gothic but also of

---

[128] Malafouris, *How Things*, p. 82.   [129] Malafouris, *How Things*, p. 82.
[130] Malafouris, *How Things*, p. 84.   [131] Malafouris, *How Things*, p. 82.
[132] Toelken, *Dynamics*, p. 37.

place – a critical component of the folkloristic process as described by nineteenth- and twentieth-century theorists of folklore and thus central to the Folk Gothic's uses of anachronistic formulations of folklore. In his important 1996 survey of folkloristics, Barre Toelken makes clear the longstanding view that folklore traditionally happens in particular locales, even as it inevitably becomes geographically dispersed (and has increasingly done so with the processes of modernisation). Toelken writes that folklore items exist in 'natural habitats', that the 'items and events of folklore are recurrent forms of *local*, dynamic human expression', reflecting 'the tastes of the *local* network of people for whom they perform'. The process of folklore, he reiterates, is thus 'local, communal', and becomes viable '*across a geographical area*'. Amplifying his discussion of the critical importance of specific place and 'natural habitat', Toelken analogises the folklore process to biological evolution: 'It is illuminating to view a traditional item or event as if it were an animal in the evolutionary process', including the importance of 'local adaptation'.[133] Animals, of course, are profoundly shaped by natural selection, as their specific environment exerts pressure on which species survive, how and in what form. Toelken's folkloric process similarly imagines a lore shaped by a specific, local geographic region. However, despite the fact that his analogue (animal evolution) inevitably highlights the centrality of place, location is in the end subordinated in Toelken's formulation to the community members who inhabit the place: folklore embodies the 'designs and values' of the people who circulate it; it reflects 'the local network of people'; it is above all 'communal'.[134] The 'folk' in the environment, not the environment itself, are highlighted as the primary if not the only *agents* in the folkloric process.

Just like things, however, place will not remain subordinated in Folk Gothic. In the Folk Gothic, the place of the agentic, determining and entrapping Gothic meets the subordinated place of the folkloric process – cast as background to the human exchange of vernacular tales and items and to the communal enactment of events. In Folk Gothic, the impersonal intrudes into the human, exerting its own indifferent, reiterative agency. This section reads Alan Garner's novel *The Owl Service* (1967) and its TV adaptation (1969–70), along with Lee Haven Jones' 2021 film *The Feast*, to argue that, in both, the very specific and necessary *place* of the folkloric process comes to the fore.

Both *The Owl Service* and *The Feast*, each set in Wales, feature the story of Blodeuwedd from the Fourth Branch of *The Mabinogion*, a collection of eleven medieval Welsh tales dating from the late fourteenth century and evolving over centuries through oral transmission before achieving written form.[135]

---

[133] Toelken, *Dynamics*, pp. 33–4, 37, 47–8   [134] Toelken, *Dynamics*, p. 34.
[135] *The Mabinogion*, trans. Sioned Davies (New York: Oxford University Press, 2007), p. 2. For a discussion of storytelling and the oral tradition in *The Mabinogion*, see pp. xiii–xvii.

As dramatised in *The Owl Service* and *The Feast*, however, this folktale is less a story exchanged by people than a story driven by the place in which it is set. The Folk Gothic of *The Owl Service* and *The Feast* enacts ecological thinking as Timothy Morton has described it: existing 'on timescales and in spatial dimensions that are profoundly inhuman',[136] everything is 'interconnected'. There is no definite background and therefore no definite foreground'.[137] Indeed, the binary of 'background' and 'foreground' dissolves into what Morton calls a constantly changing 'mesh' of 'lifeforms and non-life' – an ecological system of interconnected objects and of 'unique irreducible strange strangers' that are both human and non-human'.[138] *The Owl Service* and *The Feast* both feature 'strange strangers' embodied as women – from the folkloric Blodeuwedd to her contemporary incarnations as Alison in *The Owl Service* and Cadi in *The Feast*, each of whom stands in for the ultimately uncontrollable natural world. Each illuminates the inexorability of that underlying 'mesh' and gives agency, often violent agency, to the 'strange strangers' of the natural world; as they do so, 'people' – the 'personal and communal' of the folkloric process – waver and dissolve. In the end, the ecological Folk Gothic binds the efforts of folklore to explain and control the natural world to an ecological Gothic that drives the undoing of those efforts, disclosing the fear, dread and loss of agency at the heart of humans' encounter with nature.[139]

4.1 'Not Haunted – More Like, Still Happening'

Alan Garner's novel *The Owl Service* was published in 1967 and was then adapted by Garner as an eight-part television series for ITV, airing between 21 December 1969 and 8 February 1970. For Garner, various pieces of the story crystallised when he stayed at Bryn Hall in Llanymawddwy in Wales for a family holiday in 1960 (a place to which he returned for several years afterwards). This place, this valley, was where his story had to happen.[140]

---

[136] Timothy Morton, 'Waking up inside an Object: The Subject of Ecology', *English Language Notes*, 49:2 (Fall / Winter 2011): 183–91 (p. 190).

[137] Timothy Morton, *The Ecological Thought* (Cambridge, MA: Cambridge University Press, 2010), p. 28.

[138] Morton, 'Waking up', p. 185.

[139] This formulation draws on the extensive work on the ecoGothic, beginning with Simon Estok's formulations of ecophobia. See Simon C. Estok, *The Ecophobia Hypothesis* (New York: Routledge, 2018); Simon C. Estok, 'Theorising the EcoGothic', *Gothic Nature*, 1 (2019): 34–53, https://gothicnaturejournal.com/wp-content/uploads/2019/09/Estok_34-53_Gothic-Nature-1_2019.pdf; Dawn Keetley and Matthew Wynn Sivils (eds.), *Ecogothic in Nineteenth-Century American Literature* (New York: Routledge, 2018); and Elizabeth Parker, *The Forest and the EcoGothic: The Deep Dark Woods in the Popular Imagination* (New York: Palgrave, 2020).

[140] In the postscript to *The Owl Service*, Alan Garner writes that he 'went to stay at a house in a remote valley in North Wales. Within hours of arriving I knew that I had found the setting for

Once his characters arrive in this valley, they are unable to leave, trapped by landscape and climate, the narrative thus exemplifying Christopher Baldick's 'claustrophobic sense of *enclosure in space*'[141] – except, in its *necessary landscape*, *The Owl Service* is predicated not so much on what Baldick calls 'enclosure in space' as enclosure in a particular *place*. In this reiterated drama, the central house is enclosed by a deep valley; it stands just above a river and an ancient stone, the Stone of Gronw; at the summit of a hill on the other side of the river is a wooded copse – all are essential elements in the drama. Indeed, *The Owl Service* in every instance defies the empty flatness of 'space' in its specific topography – its country, region, climate, weather, animals, river, vegetation and rocks. And in this place, *The Owl Service* plays out the same series of events with uncanny repetition.

The place, in both the novel and the TV series, gathers the characters to it. Nancy (Dorothy Edwards) and her son Gwyn (Michael Holden), who are from the valley but have been living in Aberystwyth, are hired by the newly blended English family who are on holiday together for the first time: Margaret and her daughter Alison (Gillian Hills), who own the house, and Margaret's new husband Clive (Edwin Richfield) and his son Roger (Francis Wallis). Gwyn, Alison and Roger are then drawn ineluctably into a romantic triangle, one that has played out repeatedly before them, including an iteration enacted by Gwyn's mother Nancy, Alison's father's now-dead cousin, Bertram, and the gardener, Huw Halfbacon (Raymond Llewellyn). While this repeated story is from *The Mabinogion* – 'our national heritage' (ep. 2) – as Gwyn says to Roger and Alison – it is more accurately, in Garner's version, *from the valley*, and the valley demands its repetition. At one point, Roger asks Gwyn whether he thinks the place is haunted, and Gwyn replies: 'Not haunted - more like, still happening' (ep. 2).

The 'ancient' story told in Garner's novel and TV series is mostly true to the story as recounted in the Fourth Branch of *The Mabinogion*: two wizards or magicians, Gwydion and Math, create a wife out of flowers for Lleu Llaw Gyffes, but she falls in love with another man, Gronw Pebyr. Gronw and the wife plot to kill Lleu, and Gronw throws a spear from the top of a hill, across a river to pierce his rival. Lleu doesn't die, however, but becomes an eagle; Gwydion subsequently finds him and turns him back into a man, and he then kills Gronw in exactly the same way as Gronw attempted to kill him, by throwing a spear from the top of the hill and through a stone, which becomes

---

the story, or the setting had found me'. Alan Garner, *The Owl Service* (1967; New York: HarperCollins, 2017), p. 217. Subsequent references to *The Owl Service* will be included parenthetically in the text.

[141] Baldick, 'Introduction', p. xix; emphasis added.

known as the Stone of Gronw. To punish the woman, the wizard turns her into an owl and names her Blodeuwedd. In episode two of the TV series, Huw tells a version of this story, adding that it is not in the past but alive in the present: 'She's coming. She won't be long now.' And, 'That's how it is happening . . . all the time' (ep. 2). Alive and present in that place, the story is not banished to the past.

While different generations move through the roles of Lleu, Gronw and Blodeuwedd, the land remains. As Roger says, 'We're in the place that it happened.' In the novel, Gwyn tells Alison, after they climb the mountain above the valley, 'Listen to that river. It's what lasts . . . . It never stops. It never has stopped since it began. It was the last sound Lleu Llaw Gyffes heard before he was killed. Gronw heard it, in his turn. We hear it now' (p. 131). Hill, copse, river, stone all anchor the varied iterations, through time, of the drama of Lleu, Gronw and Blodeuwedd. Because the landscape persists while familiar linear time and the 'human' that it anchors dissolves, its role as actor comes more clearly into focus. Agency is distributed across things and land as well as humans, human and non-human is entangled, and Roger, Gwyn and Alison have little choice in their repetition of the drama of Lleu, Gronw and Blodeuwedd.

The role of non-human actors in the central drama of *The Owl Series* is evident right from the beginning of both novel and TV series. Alison is in bed, feeling poorly, when she hears a scratching in the attic above her. She sends Gwyn up to see what it is. They both presume rats, but Gwyn finds plates and brings one down to show Alison. Once given the plate, Alison starts furiously tracing the floral pattern around its border and realises that if she folds the tracing a particular way, it becomes an owl. It is clear that what Alison is doing is driven by the plates – an exterior not interior compulsion. In the TV series, this scene is intercut with shots of Roger swimming with the current of the river, another external force; the scene later cuts to Roger getting out of the river and lying on the bank, with the stone in the foreground, and when Gwyn picks up a plate in the attic, both he and Roger have a strong physical reaction – the power flowing *from objects* (plates and stone) *to them*. As Gwyn and Alison examine the plates, Roger stops to examine the stone in an intercut scene. A string of shots – from the stacked plates in the attic, to the stone as Roger explores around it, to a view of the copse through the hole in the stone, to a long shot of Roger dwarfed by the stone, river and trees – thus foregrounds all the non-human actors immanent in the valley (Figure 6). They drive the movement from one shot to the next. 'The force was in the plates. It's in us now', Gwyn says later, signalling the precedence of the plates, which is also the precedence of the stone and the land (ep. 5).

Figure 6 Roger dwarfed by stone, river and woods
Source: *The Owl Service*, directed by Peter Plummer (ITV, 1969–70), ep. 1.

Figure 7 The spirals on the Stone of Gronw
Source: *The Owl Service*, directed by Peter Plummer (ITV, 1969–70), ep. 3.

Of the agentic elements that make up 'place' in *The Owl Service*, the most prominent, especially as visually rendered in the TV series, is the Stone of Gronw. The looping recursivity of Folk Gothic's ecological time is evident in the camera's return to this stone and amplified by the spirals etched across its surface (Figure 7). These marks symbolise a looping repetition (albeit along linear time). They also signal a different way of understanding the agency driving the recursive plot of *The Owl Service*. Describing his 'Material

Engagement Theory', archaeologist Lambros Malafouris articulates a conception of memory that is constituted by an interwoven human and non-human, and he discusses marks on Mycenaean tablets as illustrative of 'cognitive artifacts'. These artefacts do not just serve as an (external) archive of memories forged in the human brain; rather, they both '*constitute* our memories' and '*have memories of their own*', he claims.[142] Memory, then, is not limited to and bounded by the human mind, brain and body; it is instead a 'cognitive system' that includes things.[143] Within this 'system's viewpoint', it is actually not the engraver who remembers but the engraved tablet or stone. In transcending the biological limitation of the individual person, memories thus become available '"out there" for other people to use, comment on, transform, or incorporate'.[144] In the context of depictions of non-human objects as having memory in the Folk Gothic, however, it's not only humans who 'use' artefacts to remember; artefacts just as readily 'use, comment on, transform, or incorporate' the human.[145] Indeed, in *The Owl Service*, whoever may have etched the symbols on the Stone of Gronw is not only long gone but not even mentioned or considered. Instead, the stone itself holds the memory. This memory, moreover, seeps from stone to human and in large part drives their actions; it is akin to muscle memory (because it is unconscious, involuntary), but it is located in matter beyond the body. It is *stone memory* or, more generally, object memory. 'We're in the place that it happened', Roger says, referring to the stone (ep. 2) – and he will soon find that 'place' becomes intermeshed with his interiority.

The mesh of human and non-human that drives the recurring iterations of the story of Lleu, Gronw and Blodeuwedd is not only composed of plates, stone, spear, and river. The animals, topography and weather of the valley are all integral parts of the agentic 'assemblage' of human and non-human – what Jane Bennett has aptly defined as the 'ontologically heterogeneous field' across which 'force' (agency) is 'distributed'.[146] Both Gwyn and Nancy try to leave at various points, but the valley resists. Indeed, they are hampered, and in Gwyn's case prevented, by the valley itself. Garner's novel includes scenes slightly truncated in the TV series in which Gwyn is stopped from leaving the valley by, successively, dogs (pp. 164–8), a shale buttress and waterfall (pp. 175–6), boulders (p. 176), a black sow (p. 177), and Huw (pp. 180–6). Later on, in both the novel and the TV series, when Nancy leaves and tries to drag Gwyn with her, they are hindered by sheeting rain, a deluge that continues through the end of the series, and that Garner centrally features in his novel: 'the

---

[142] Malafouris, *How Things*, p. 67, p. 80; emphasis added.
[143] Malafouris, *How Things*, pp. 80–1. [144] Malafouris, *How Things*, p. 82.
[145] Malafouris, *How Things*, p. 82. [146] Bennett, *Vibrant Matter*, p. 23.

rain fell in solid rods of water', he writes (p. 193). The rain is so forceful, it appears animate: Gwyn 'had never seen rain spread visible in the sky, and its life was something he could feel as it dropped between him and the mountains' (p. 196). When Roger sees Huw outside with Alison near the novel's conclusion, 'The rain moved behind him, the earth boiled as if under a harrow' (p. 207). And the climactic scene of the novel takes place in inchoate sound, 'hard to place among the trees, and the rain and the river crashed in flood'; it was 'the noise of a wind on the pass and its echo before it in the valley, or it was the noise of owls hunting' (p. 209). Visually and aurally, the sheets of rain displace the characters' priority in the frame of the TV series, something Garner beautifully articulates in the novel as Nancy struggles away: her 'haunted' face is 'dissolved', Garner writes, the 'dark line of her' – her separate identity – broken by the rain 'into webs that left no stain' (p. 202). The human becomes literally dissolved into the 'web' that also encompasses everything – every 'thing', distinctive yet interconnected – in the valley.

In *The Owl Service*, however, the power of place stands in overt tension with the explicable anthropocentric, as human presence and purpose struggle to supersede the force of place. A portrait of Blodeuwedd that features prominently in the novel and the TV series represents this tension. As a portrait, it by definition foregrounds the human – both visually and in how it is described in the novel: 'The woman was painted life-size in oils on wooden panelling. She stood against a background of clover heads spaced in rows' (p. 39; see Figure 8). And yet, when the characters discover the painting, their attention almost immediately moves to that background, as their attention is drawn to the clover

Figure 8 The portrait of Blodeuwedd
Source: *The Owl Service*, directed by Peter Plummer (ITV, 1969–70), ep. 3.

heads, which they discover are actually claws that only look like petals (p. 41). The figure dissolves into its own background, then, into the petals and claws that shape the recurring story into Garner's 'webs' of the non-human (p. 202).

Human agency in *The Owl Service* is structured by gender, as women (Blodeuwedd, Alison, Nancy) are much more frequently entangled with a non-human 'background'. This gendered anthropocentrism is evident in *The Mabinogion* itself, with its own foregrounding of masculine characters and motive. The origin of the Lleu-Gronw-Blodeuwedd triangle, after all, is the 'wizard' Gwydion who 'made the wife out of flowers' for Lleu. In this plot, nature is shaped by a creator and thus rendered passive and plastic. Gwyn describes the 'wizard' in starkly human (and agential) terms when he says to Alison, 'Suppose *someone* found power in this valley – *made* a woman out of flowers' (ep. 5; emphasis added). Huw is at times the wizard Gwydion, even as he also figures as one of the lovers in the triangle of the earlier generation (with Nancy and Bertram). As Gwydion, he proclaims: 'I own the ground, the mountain, the valley, the sound of the cuckoo, the brambles, the berries, the dark cave is mine . . . I am a fire upon a hill, I am a hawk, I am a wolf . . . *I am*' (ep. 3). That Huw embodies the all-powerful wizard locates agency in a male body, one that contains and suppresses the force of the (feminised) non-human.

Roger accrues some of the power of Gwydion/Huw through his hobby of photography. Despite the opening shots of Roger carried by the river's current and the long shot of him dwarfed by the Stone of Gronw, the opening of the first episode also includes a shot in which he looks through the hole and sees the copse. Unlike the spirals etched *on* the stone, which figure the non-human, when Roger looks *through* the stone, *his* point of view dominates. 'I want to use the rock texture as a frame for the trees in the distance', he tells Gwyn. 'It should make an interesting composition' (p. 64). Later, talking to his father about his photographs of the stone, Roger says, 'the different shades are because *I* gave them different exposures – but you can see how *I've* made the hole frame the trees on the Bryn' (p. 105; emphasis added). In Roger's regular emphasis on his 'compositions' of the objects around him, he draws the stone into a passive role in human action, whether that action is spear-throwing, photography or mere looking; the stone is not alone, silent, in the landscape.

The power of human action and intention in *The Owl Series* becomes most evident in the ending of both the novel and the series, an ending that asserts not only human but more specifically male and English agency. Alison is in pain, with scratches on her body, and Huw says, 'Always it is owls, always we are destroyed. Why must she see owls and not flowers? Always it is the same' (p. 211). In an act of loving generosity of which Gwyn is expressly incapable, Roger goes to Alison and tells her, 'She's not owls. She's flowers. Flowers. Flowers, Ali', stroking her forehead (p. 213). As he keeps reassuring Alison, she calms and the scratches disappear. The novel concludes with petals falling from above. Critics have read the ending as an assertion of distinctly human agency. Neil Philip, for instance, has posited that this ending is 'the moment at which Garner casts aside the Fourth Branch and sets his characters free'.[147] That 'freedom', however, is granted only to Roger, not to Alison. Dimitra Fimi writes that, despite their 'ability to possess and destroy', Blodeuwedd (and Alison) 'are ultimately controlled by the male characters in the novel'.[148] Cara Bartels–Bland also emphasises Alison's lack of agency: 'Alison is unable to choose herself, because she has succumbed to the possession of Blodeuwedd, so, through their own decisions, the male protagonists Gwyn and Roger determine her fate for her'.[149] It is telling, moreover, that the English Roger and not the Welsh Gwyn saves Alison: this particular cycle of the Welsh myth thus ends with the two English characters breaking a cycle that has persistently trapped its Welsh characters. In entering the valley as interlopers and then extricating themselves from the continual pattern of destruction rooted in the land, Roger and Alison not only possess a freedom that the doomed Welsh characters seem powerless to exert but also a form of dominance that continues centuries of English colonial power over Wales. They exert the repeated 'conquest' of Wales that Jane Aaron has argued is at the heart of Welsh Gothic.[150]

Significantly, the television series doesn't end where the novel does. It cuts back to the river and then to three children (two boys and a girl) who are speaking Welsh, telling (again) the story of Blodeuwedd, Lleu and Gronw. As the camera pulls back, we see that they are framed through the hole in the Stone of Gronw, and this shot continues for a significant length of time. This shot is distinctly free of Roger's gaze, free of his control of the stone, of his 'composing'. Here, the gaze through the hole in the stone is impersonal, dislodged from the anthropocentrism and both the English and the male control of the cycle that is, in the end, enacted in Garner's novel.

4.2 Blodeuwedd's Feast

In Lee Haven Jones' 2021 Welsh cinematic version of the story of Blodeuwedd, *The Feast*, Blodeuwedd becomes a very different kind of character. Taking over the body of a woman who dies off-screen at the beginning of the film,

---

[147] Neil Philip, *A Fine Anger: A Critical Introduction to the Work of Alan Garner* (New York: Philomel Books, 1981), p.71.

[148] Dimitra Fimi, *Celtic Myth in Contemporary Children's Fantasy: Idealization, Identity, Ideology* (New York: Palgrave Macmillan, 2017), pp. 161–2.

[149] Cara Bartels–Bland, '"You Took My Spirit Captive among the Leaves': The Creation of Blodeuwedd in Re-Imaginings of the Fourth Branch of the *Mabinogi*', *The Pomegranate: The International Journal of Pagan Studies*, 16:2 (2014): 178–206 (p. 195).

[150] Jane Aaron, *Welsh Gothic* (Cardiff: University of Wales Press, 2013), p. 1.

Blodeuwedd as Cadi (Annes Elwy) actively resists the familiar, anthropocentric love plot. She is, moreover, much more than Alison, profoundly interwoven with nature. Despite her possession by Blodeuwedd, Alison remains alienated from the valley. As she tells Gwyn (in a line repeated in the television series), 'I'm as useless as one of those girls in fashion photographs – just stuck in a field of wheat, or a puddle, or on a mountain, and they look gorgeous but they don't know where they are. I'm like that. I don't belong' (p. 98; ep. 4). In *The Feast*, on the other hand, Cadi is not incongruously 'stuck in' nature; she *is* nature; she is fields, vegetation and mountain; she belongs. Later in the film, she will roll ecstatically in the earth while roots and grass reach towards her, acknowledging kinship. While Alison ends up being a figure of female passivity and English usurpation, then, imposed *on* a static landscape. Cadi is a part *of* the animate earth, arisen to avenge the depredations of modernity and the exploitation of Welsh land. Tellingly, actor Annes Elwy calls Cadi a 'creature' – silent and sensual and never entirely human.[151]

If Garner's novel engages in a problematic, if covert, colonisation of Welsh characters, history and folklore, Lee Haven Jones expressly seeks to counter such efforts in *The Feast*, saying in an interview that he wants his work 'to challenge the suppression of the Welsh language in the global marketplace',[152] something the television adaptation of *The Owl Service* seems to espouse only in its very ending. Like Garner's *The Owl Service*, Jones has claimed that his film is influenced by *The Mabinogion*, which he describes as 'a series of folk tales, legends, and myths' that are 'full of horrific things'.[153] Articulating that influence more fully in another interview, Jones noted that *The Feast* is predicated on a 'real folktale', continuing:

> It's based very loosely on a material called Blodeuwedd, which comes from **The Mabinogion** which is the oldest existing piece of literature in the British Isles. It's a story about a girl who basically is made of flowers. So as ever, there are all sorts of curses involved. There's a prince who has a rather wicked mother, who says you will never have a wife from amongst human beings, so his wizard friend creates this woman out of flowers and harnesses the spirit of nature (cue Cadi!) and then of course it all goes terribly wrong because she is an embodiment of nature and doesn't want to be captured in a body like that.[154]

[151] 'The Feast, Interview with Lee Haven Jones and Annes Elwy', British Independent Film Awards, YouTube, 18 August 2022, https://youtu.be/IPTNkDbTobY [last accessed 10 February 2023].

[152] Paul Risker, 'Horror Is a Trojan Horse in Welsh Director Lee Haven Jones' "The Feast"', *PopMatters*, 1 December 2021, www.popmatters.com/lee-haven-jones-director-interview [last accessed 5 February 2023].

[153] Risker, 'Horror'.

[154] Rachel Harper, 'The Feast: Horror in the Welsh Countryside', *SciFiNow*, 19 August 2022, www.scifinow.co.uk/cinema/the-feast-horror-in-the-welsh-countryside/ [last accessed 10 February 2023].

Jones here articulates not just his intent to centre a specifically Welsh legend but also what is largely unrealised in *The Owl Service*: Blodeuwedd's hybrid human–non-human nature, her birth from flowers, her 'embodiment of nature'. This fact, as Jones makes clear, is central to *The Feast*.

In tracing the story of Blodeuwedd in *The Mabinogion*, *The Feast* inevitably evinces some similarities with *The Owl Service*. Both take place in a rural part of Wales and both feature a family that is alienated from the land they're inhabiting. In *The Owl Service*, the principal family (Clive, Margaret, Roger, and Alison) are English; in *The Feast*, the family is Welsh by nationality, but they nonetheless reject that identity and place. Gwyn (Julian Lewis Jones) is a politician, and he and his wife Glenda (Nia Roberts), spend as much time as possible in London. Gwyn and Glenda's two sons, Guto (Steffan Cennydd) and Gweirydd (Sion Alun Davies) also find ways to remove themselves from a place they loathe. Echoing the desire of Gwyn in *The Owl Service* to return to Aberystwyth, Guto tells Cadi that London is the only place he wants to live. When Cadi arrives at the house, ostensibly as the waitress Glenda hired for the evening's dinner party, she initiates a 'love triangle' that echoes that of Gwyn, Roger and Alison and, before that, of Lleu, Gronw and Blodeuwedd. Indeed, Guto seems immediately attracted to Cadi and says they should run away to London together. Cadi will later have sex in the woods with his brother Gweirydd, but only to ensure that he dies a gruesome death. Indeed, as the film progresses, Cadi begins enacting the violence only suggestively evoked in *The Owl Service*, with Blodeuwedd's (and Alison's) 'claws' – claws Alison rarely used. Cadi, however, is all 'claws': she kills Gwyn, Gluto and Gweirydd and seemingly passes her destructive power to Glenda. Of all her family, Glenda is the most connected to the land and local lore. In one scene, a red feather (suggestive of owls and blood) floats down by her, indicating that she too may have some of Blodeuwedd in her – and, indeed, she ultimately kills their dinner guest, Euros (Rhodri Meilir), exemplary capitalist, and then herself.

Gwyn and Glenda's dinner party is integral to their plan to exploit the land and is thus the reason that *The Feast*'s incarnation of Blodeuwedd is awoken. The film implies that while Blodeuwedd may take Cadi's form in this moment, she has always been present in that place. Cadi returns because her 'home', the Rise, has been disturbed by mining, as becomes clear in a critical conversation between Glenda and her neighbour Mair (Lisa Palfrey), both of whom grew up in the area. Glenda tells Mair that she and Gwyn invited Mair and her husband to dinner so that they could meet Euros, a developer who has already made a significant amount of money for them. But he has recently found 'something' that crosses into Mair's property: 'they suspect the vein runs through your farm all the way west', Glenda says. The developers are ultimately interested, Glenda adds bluntly, in 'the Rise'. Mair looks at Glenda in disbelief: 'We don't farm the Rise', she says, 'Leave the Rise alone. That's what everyone has done'.

Glenda: You're not superstitious?
Mair: You know the story.
Glenda: A legend!
Mair: That's where she's resting, Glenda.
Glenda: That's what the adults said to keep us kids from wandering.
Mair: She shouldn't be awakened.
Glenda: Nonsense. And shame on you for believing it.

As the two women talk, they stand in front of an abstract painting that has dominated interior scenes of the house (Figure 9). When Glenda mentions that the developers are interested in the Rise, she points to the black shapes near the bottom right of the painting – dark, uncharted terrain, uncharted precisely because the unnamed 'she' is resting there. And it is from this unmapped terrain that Cadi has returned, embodying the 'she' of local folklore.

As Glenda and Mair discuss local folklore late in the film, the significance of the film's opening scene becomes clear. The film begins with a shot of a drill in open land; then we see the worker operating it staggering away towards the camera, covered in blood. At the dinner party, later, Euros tells Gwyn that a worker became 'ill' at an exploratory site that morning – presumably on the 'Rise'. Euros goes on to say that the drill went deeper than usual, breaking through to a cave system, and he shows the pictures to Gwyn. He adds that, there's 'no record of caves in the area. It contradicts all the geological informa-tion they have'. He is organising a 'team of climbers to go there to find out

Figure 9 The abstract painting that represents the house and surrounding area
Source: *The Feast*, directed by Lee Haven Jones (Sgrech, 2021).

Figure 10 The map of the land and its mining sites
Source: *The Feast*, directed by Lee Haven Jones (Sgrech, 2021).

more'. Unaware of or unconcerned with local folklore, Euros avidly pursues potential resources on the 'sacred' ground of the Rise.

As Euros tells Gwyn about the exploratory mining site, he shows him a map of the area: red triangles 'represent the sites that are yet to be explored; yellow, the sites that haven't shown potential; and green sites where minerals and valuable metals have been discovered already'. The black square is Gwyn and Glenda's house, and the blue triangle signifies the newly discovered cave system. This map, with its non-representational colours and shapes serves to abstract the land in the same way that Glenda's painting does (Figure 10). Both seek to represent the region and yet are profoundly detached from it. In this detachment, moreover, they serve to represent the region in ways that make it legible within the web of global capitalism, rendering it readable to investors and developers around the world and wrenching it from local land and lore. That it is merely a node in the abstract web of capitalist modernity is precisely what is wrong with the house itself, in all its newness. Glenda tells Cadi how the farm that had long stood in that place was recently demolished, replaced by their current house, which took two years to build. Glenda says that she stored some of her 'things' when they moved out of the farm, but that they 'don't suit the place now. They feel primitive', she adds, articulating a fundamental binary of the film, which is structured between abstract modernity and a more tangible and grounded 'primitive'. In its abstract modernity, the house echoes the painting and the developer's map, forming a nexus of capitalist abstraction and extraction. It is precisely to thwart this abstraction that Cadi returns, in all her mute and earthly 'primitiveness'.

Embodying the centrality of the valley itself to *The Owl Service*, both the house in north Wales that inspired Garner to write the novel and the house in

Cheshire in which the television series was filmed were both rooted in local place.[155] The house in which *The Feast* was filmed – the 'Life House' near Llanbister in mid Wales – has a much a different relation to its location, however.[156] For the most part, the house is not of the place but against it – something not entirely evident at first, since one of the most striking features of the house is its windows, which open it up to the space outside. Architect and critic, Kenneth Frampton, writes that windows have 'an innate capacity to inscribe architecture with the character of a region and hence to express the place in which the work is situated'.[157] The narrative of *The Feast* works against this embeddedness in place, however, as the family who lives in the house is thoroughly detached from it, even in their adjacency to windows. The windows serve either as ways of framing a 'nature' from which the family is thoroughly alienated or as mirrors that fail to offer passage to the outside, reflecting instead only what is inside. In one scene, Guto sits by the window staring at a cut on his foot, not out the window, and the fact that he is much more interested in looking at himself than what is outside is amplified by the window's offering up his reflection. Gweirydd, who is obsessed with his body, stands for an excruciatingly long scene admiring himself in a mirror in his well-lit bedroom. The natural light from the large windows right next to him bathe the scene, but he ignores what is beyond the windows to focus only on his own reflection in the mirror.

Once the titular 'feast' begins, even the characters' proximity to windows and the land beyond ceases, and most of the rest of the film presents the house as enclosed – claustrophobic. When Glenda takes Mair on a tour of the house, she shows her the windowless room where she goes to 'relax, meditate', but Mair replies, in horror, 'It's like a cell'. The double-meaning of 'cell' comes into play

---

[155] Bryn Hall in Llanymawddwy, near Dinas Mawddwy, where Garner went on holiday with his family and from where he drew inspiration for *The Owl Service*, was built in the seventeenth century 'of roughly coursed *local* rubble, with a slate roof' – slate being a longstanding industry of (especially) north Wales (back to the Roman era). 'Bryn Hall', *British Listed Buildings*, [n.d.], https://britishlistedbuildings.co.uk/300022624-bryn-hall-mawddwy [last accessed 17 February 2023]. Poulton Hall in Wirral, Cheshire, where the TV series was filmed also dates back to the seventeenth century, although a fourteenth-century house stood on the same site and, before that, reputedly, an (at least) eleventh-century castle. The current house incorporates older materials from earlier locations – notably its cellar is partly composed of the stones of the castle – and it also contains a stair with balusters, 'believed to be taken from the altar rail at [the nearby] Lower Bebington Church'. 'Poulton Hall', *Historic Houses*, [n.d.], www.historichouses.org/house/poulton-hall/visit/ [last accessed 17 February 2023]; 'Poulton Hall', *British Listed Buildings*, [n.d.], https://britishlistedbuildings.co.uk/101343498-poulton-hall-clatterbridge-ward [last accessed 17 February 2023].

[156] See the description of the Life House on John Pawson's website, www.johnpawson.com/works/life-house [last accessed 19 February 2023].

[157] Kenneth Frampton, 'Towards a Critical Regionalism: Six Points for an Architecture of Resistance', in Hal Foster (ed.), *The Anti-Aesthetic: Essays on Postmodern Culture* (Port Townsend, WA: Bay Press, 1983), pp. 16–30 (p. 26).

here (prison cell, monastic cell), as the house was actually designed for meditation. Architect John Pawson's website describes how the spatial arrangement of the house shares 'characteristics with the monastic cloister' and that the rooms were designed 'with the idea of supporting and enriching specific rituals'. Glenda, Guto and Gweirydd all do, in fact, engage in ritualistic behaviour – but the principal deity the family worships, the deity to whom their rituals are devoted, is themselves.

The house in *The Feast* also articulates an antagonistic relationship with the land in that it is not (in both its real and fictional incarnations) made from local materials. The director has said, 'It's such a cliché to say that the location is a character, but it's more than that: it's a metaphor for the family, a physical manifestation of their relationships'.[158] The principal attribute of the family that the house mirrors, with its imported materials, is precisely their detachment from local place. An article in prominent architectural magazine, *Dezeen*, notes that the Life House was made from expensive and imported Danish brick[159] popular with high-end architects, despite the fact that Wales has its own rich brickmaking and masonry tradition.[160] Reflecting the conditions of the house in which the film is shot, Glenda tells Mair that the 'architect was keen to source the best materials. He tried to buy locally, but it wasn't always possible'. Like the architect, Glenda herself gives only lip service to the importance of the local. As she unpacks food delivered by a courier for her 'feast', she tells Cadi that 'the local supermarket is fine for everyday items, but you won't find bok choy on its shelves'. You also won't find the array of tropical fruit she has ordered – mango, pineapple, pomegranate, kiwi – some of which she offers to Cadi, who grimaces in disgust when she tries it. Embodiment of the local, Cadi will not tolerate food imported from afar. Both the family and their house, however, are fully invested in the import, inextricably parts of a web of global materials, products and investments.

At the end of *The Feast*, the family – imbricated in a web of international capital and extractive development – is dead. Cadi kills the men (Gwyn, Guto and Gweiryyd) – all of whom express some disturbing form of sexual interest in her, all some version of Lleu, the husband for whom Blodeuwedd is 'made' and then forced to marry in *The Mabinogion*. (Cadi overtly refuses such enforced bonds.)

---

[158] As soon as Jones and Williams found the house, they knew they had found the perfect house for the film, and they began rewriting parts of the screenplay to account for it. See Nikki Baughan, 'How we made Welsh horror The Feast: "I was trying to craft something specifically not English"', *BFI*, 16 August 2022, www.bfi.org.uk/interviews/feast-lee-haven-jones [last accessed 19 February 2023].

[159] Amy Frearson, 'John Pawson's Life House is a Welsh Countryside Retreat Built from Dark and Light Bricks', *Dezeen*, 22 April 2016, www.dezeen.com/2016/04/22/life-house-john-pawson-living-architecture-alain-de-botton-brick-holiday-home-wales/ [last accessed 19 February 2023].

[160] I want to thank Dr Wesley Hiatt, a professor of architecture at Lehigh University, for pointing out the irony of the Danish brick used to build a house in a country known for its brick-making tradition.

Then Glenda kills Euros. 'After you've taken everything', Glenda asks Euros, 'what will be left?' – a question she could and does turn on herself, killing herself after shooting Euros. It is not only this family whom Cadi kills, however. She kills the drill operator at the beginning of the film – and she comes to inhabit Cadi's body after she kills both her and her father, a man who happens to work for a company building wind turbines and who was driving a truck carrying parts for those turbines. The spirit incarnate in Cadi is inimical to any kind of development, representing Jones' desire to make a film that was not only distinctively Welsh but also about the global 'climate crisis'. *The Feast* is, he has said, 'this message about environmentalism and sustainability, about how we use the land and abuse the earth'.[161]

Although Jones has talked in interviews about *The Mabinogion*, specifically the story of Blodeuwedd, as the inspiration for his film, neither is actually mentioned in the film itself. In this way, *The Feast* is very much unlike Alan Garner's *The Owl Service* and its television adaptation, both of which repeatedly and explicitly tell the story of Blodeuwedd, Lleu and Gronw. *The Feast* strips this original tale from its diegesis, centring Cadi as the embodiment of folklore that remains largely unspoken. In its most direct invocation, the film has Mair warn Glenda that the Rise is 'where she's resting', and that she 'shouldn't be awakened'. The red feather that floats down by Glenda when she and Mair are in her 'cell' hints at Blodeuwedd's transformation into an owl in *The Mabinogion*, although, again, she is not named. In its backgrounding of the folklore itself, *The Feast* reveals with all the more clarity that what underlies it is the land. Cadi does not speak throughout the film, although she does at one point sing a local folk song. Cadi is silent because she is nature itself. She rolls on the earth; she caresses a tree as she picks fungi for Gudo. When she sees Glenda's painting of the local region, she doesn't look at it, she is not detached, despite the impetus of the painting itself; rather, she presses herself against it, just as she does with trees, grass, and earth – and they move towards her as she does to them. And when Cadi touches the 'pure' white objects in Glenda's house, she leaves tracks of dirt: she is dirt, is earth.

Garner's novel represented the efficacy of non-human actors and made clear the ways in which the myth of Blodeuwedd, indeed Blodeuwedd herself, was inextricable from nature, from the mountain, from flowers and owls, river and stone. In the end, though, Garner subordinated this story to human agency, validating the 'freedom' of at least some humans. *The Feast*, on the other hand, makes the local place – the mountain, the earth – incarnate in Cadi; she is silent, profoundly and expressly intertwined with dirt, vegetation, the land itself, and

---

[161] Baughan, 'How We Made'; Risker, 'Horror'.

she is above all a powerful actor. Every impulse of the central characters of this film – what they do, their house, their art, their drive to develop all the land around them – is designed to distance themselves from the land and to control the non-human. *The Feast*'s Cadi – a folkloric figure stripped of the human appurtenances of folklore, embodying the place itself, the land that undergirds that folklore – shows them that they cannot live that way.

Bibliography

Aaron, Jane, *Welsh Gothic* (Cardiff: University of Wales Press, 2013).

Abrahams, Roger D., 'Phantoms of Romantic Nationalism in Folkloristics', *The Journal of American Folklore*, 106:419 (Winter 1993): 3–37.

Aguirre, Manuel, 'Gothic Fiction and Folk-Narrative Structure: The Case of Mary Shelley's *Frankenstein*', *Gothic Studies*, 15:2 (November 2013): 1–18.

Aldana Reyes, Xavier, *Gothic Cinema* (New York: Routledge, 2020).

Altman, Rick, *The American Musical Film* (Bloomington, IN: Indiana University Press, 1987).

Baldick, Chris, 'Introduction', in Chris Baldick (ed.), *The Oxford Book of Gothic Tales* (New York: Oxford University Press, 1993), pp. xi – xxiii.

Ben-Amos, Dan, 'Toward a Definition of Folklore in Context', in Américo Paredes and Richard Bauman (eds.), *Toward New Perspectives in Folklore* (1972; Bloomington, IN: Trickster Press, 2000), pp. 3–19.

Bennett, Jane, *Vibrant Matter: A Political Ecology of Things* (Durham, NC: Duke University Press, 2010).

Benson, Edward Frederic, 'The Flint Knife', in Mike Ashley (ed.), *The Outcast and Other Dark Tales by E. F. Benson* (London: The British Library, 2020), pp. 209–23.

Benson, Edward Frederic, 'The Temple', in *Night Terrors: The Ghost Stories of E. F. Benson* (Ware: Wordsworth Editions, 2012), pp. 517–31.

Blackwood, Algernon, 'Ancient Sorceries', in S. T. Joshi (ed.), *Ancient Sorceries and Other Weird Tales* (New York: Penguin, 2002), pp. 87–130.

Botting, Fred, 'Dark Materialism: Gothic Objects, Commodities and Things', in Jerrold E. Hogle and Robert Miles (eds.), *The Gothic and Theory: An Edinburgh Companion* (Edinburgh: Edinburgh University Press, 2019), pp. 240–59.

Botting, Fred, *Gothic* (New York: Routledge, 1996).

Bronner, Simon J., *Folklore: The Basics* (New York: Routledge, 2017).

Bronner, Simon J., (ed.), *The Meaning of Folklore: The Analytical Essays of Alan Dundes* (Logan, UT: Utah State University Press, 2007).

Brown, Bill, 'The Tyranny of Things (Trivia in Karl Marx and Mark Twain)', *Critical Inquiry*, 28:2 (Winter 2002): 442–69.

Brown, Bill, 'Thing Theory', *Critical Inquiry*, 28:1 (Autumn 2001): 1–22.

Budzinski, Nathaniel, '"It's All an Indian Burial Ground": Folk Horror Cinema's Reckoning with Colonial Violence', *ArtReview*, 10 December

2021, https://artreview.com/its-all-an-indian-burial-ground-folk-horror-cin ema-reckoning-with-colonial-violence/.

Carroll, Noël, *The Philosophy of Horror; or, Paradoxes of the Heart* (New York: Routledge, 1990).

Chambers, Jamie, 'Troubling Folk Horror: Exoticism, Metonymy, and Solipsism in the "Unholy Trinity" and Beyond', *JCMS: Journal of Cinema and Media Studies*, 61:2 (Winter 2022): 9–34.

Clasen, Mathias, *Why Horror Seduces* (New York: Oxford University Press, 2017).

Cohen, Jeffrey Jerome, *Stone: An Ecology of the Inhuman* (Minneapolis, MN: University of Minnesota Press, 2015).

Cowdell, Paul, '"Practising Witchcraft Myself during the Filming": Folk Horror, Folklore, and the Folkloresque', *Western Folklore*, 78:4 (Fall 2019): 295–326.

The Descent, directed by Neil Marshall (Celador Films, 2005).

Dundes, Alan, *Interpreting Folklore* (Bloomington, IN: Indiana University Press, 1980).

Estok, Simon C., 'Theorising the EcoGothic', *Gothic Nature*, 1 (2019): 34–53.

Estok, Simon C., *The Ecophobia Hypothesis* (New York: Routledge, 2018).

The Feast, directed by Lee Haven Jones (Sgrech, 2021).

Fisher, Mark, *The Weird and the Eerie* (London: Repeater Books, 2016).

Foster, Michael Dylan, and Jeffrey A. Tolbert (eds.), *The Folkloresque: Reframing Folklore in a Popular Culture World* (Logan, UT: Utah State University Press, 2015).

Frampton, Kenneth, 'Towards a Critical Regionalism: Six Points for an Architecture of Resistance', in Hal Foster (ed.), *The Anti-Aesthetic: Essays on Postmodern Culture* (Port Townsend, WA: Bay Press, 1983), pp. 16–30.

Freeland, Cynthia, 'Horror and Art-Dread', in Stephen Prince (ed.), *The Horror Film* (New York: Routledge, 2004), pp. 189–205.

Garner, Alan, *The Owl Service* (1967; New York: HarperCollins, 2017).

Gelder, Ken, *Reading the Vampire* (New York: Routledge, 1994).

Goodhart, David, *The Road to Somewhere: The Populist Revolt and the Future of Politics* (London: Hurst, 2017).

The Green Inferno, directed by Eli Roth (Worldview Entertainment, 2013).

Hart, Carina, 'Gothic Folklore and Fairy Tale: Negative Nostalgia', *Gothic Studies*, 22:1 (2020): 1–13.

Heholt, Ruth, 'Sunny Landscapes, Dark Visions: E. F. Benson's Weird Domestic Folk Horror', in Dawn Keetley and Ruth Heholt (eds.), *Folk Horror: New Global Pathways* (Cardiff: University of Wales Press, 2023), pp. 145–65.

In the Earth, directed by Ben Wheatley (Rook Films, 2021).

Joy, Eileen A., 'Weird Reading', *Speculations: A Journal of Speculative Realism*, 4 (2013): 28–34.

Keetley, Dawn, 'Defining Folk Horror', *Revenant: Critical and Creative Studies of the Supernatural*, 5 (March 2020): 1–32.

Keetley, Dawn, 'Dislodged Anthropocentrism and Ecological Critique in Folk Horror: From "Children of the Corn" and *The Wicker Man* to "In the Tall Grass" and *Children of the Stones*', *Gothic Nature*, 2 (Winter 2021): 13–36.

Keetley, Dawn, 'Sacrifice Zones in Appalachian Folk Horror', in Dawn Keetley and Ruth Heholt (eds.), *Folk Horror: New Global Pathways* (Cardiff: University of Wales Press, 2023), pp. 245–61.

Keetley, Dawn, '*True Detective*'s Folk Gothic', in Justin Edwards, Rune Graulund and Johan Höglund (eds.), *Dark Scenes from Damaged Earth: The Gothic Anthropocene* (Minneapolis, MN: University of Minnesota Press, 2022), pp. 130–50.

Keetley, Dawn, and Ruth Heholt (eds.), *Folk Horror: New Global Pathways* (Cardiff: University of Wales Press, 2023).

Koven, Mikel J., *Film, Folklore, and Urban Legends* (Lanham, MD: The Scarecrow Press, 2008).

Malafouris, Lambros, *How Things Shape the Mind: A Theory of Material Engagement* (Cambridge, MA: The MIT Press, 2013).

McDonald, Keith, and Wayne Johnson, *Contemporary Gothic and Horror Film* (London: Anthem Press, 2021).

McDowell, Stacey, 'Folklore', in William Hughes, David Punter and Andrew Smith (eds.), *The Encyclopedia of the Gothic* (Malden, MA: Wiley-Blackwell, 2016), pp. 252–4.

Midsommar, directed by Ari Aster (Square Peg, 2019).

Morton, Timothy, *The Ecological Thought* (Cambridge, MA: Cambridge University Press, 2010).

Morton, Timothy, 'Waking up inside an Object: The Subject of Ecology', *English Language Notes*, 49:2 (Fall / Winter 2011): 183–91.

Mullen, Lisa, *Mid-Century Gothic: The Uncanny Objects of Modernity in British Literature and Culture after the Second World War* (Manchester: Manchester University Press, 2019).

Murphy, Bernice M., 'Folk Horror', in Stephen Shapiro and Mark Storey (eds.), *The Cambridge Companion to American Horror* (New York: Cambridge University Press, 2022), pp. 139–53.

Neale, Steve, *Genre and Hollywood* (New York: Routledge, 2000).

Newland, Paul, 'Folk Horror and the Contemporary Cult of British Rural Landscape: The Case of *Blood on Satan's Claw*', in Paul Newland (ed.),

British Landscapes on Film (Manchester: Manchester University Press, 2016), pp. 162–79.

Oring, Elliott, 'On the Concepts of Folklore', in Elliott Oring (ed.), *Folk Groups and Folklore Genres: An Introduction* (Logan, UT: Utah State University Press, 1986), pp. 1–22.

The Owl Service, directed by Peter Plummer (ITV, 1969–70).

Parker, Elizabeth, *The Forest and the EcoGothic: The Deep Dark Woods in the Popular Imagination* (New York: Palgrave, 2020).

Pet Sematary, directed by Mary Lambert (Paramount, 1989).

The Ritual, directed by David Bruckner (The Imaginarium, 2017).

Scott, Eleanor, 'Randalls Round', in Aaron Worth (ed.), *Randalls Round: Nine Nightmares* (London: The British Library, 2021), pp. 21–37.

Scovell, Adam, *Folk Horror: Hours Dreadful and Things Strange* (Leighton Buzzard: Auteur, 2017).

Stephenson, Barry, *Ritual: A Very Short Introduction* (New York: Oxford University Press, 2015).

Thurgill, James, 'The Fear of the Folk: On *Topophobia* and the Horror of Rural Landscapes', *Revenant: Critical and Creative Studies of the Supernatural*, 5 (2020): 33–56.

Toelken, Barre, *The Dynamics of Folklore* (Logan, UT: Utah State University Press, 1996).

Tolbert, Jeffrey A., 'The Frightening Folk: An Introduction to the Folkloresque in Horror', in Dawn Keetley and Ruth Heholt (eds.), *Folk Horror: New Global Pathways* (Cardiff: University of Wales Press, 2023), pp. 25–41.

Veracini, Lorenzo, *Settler Colonialism: A Theoretical Overview* (London: Palgrave Macmillan, 2010).

Vieira, Mark A., *Hollywood Horror: From Gothic to Cosmic* (New York: Harry N. Abrams, 2003).

Walsham, Alexandra, *The Reformation of the Landscape: Religion, Identity, and Memory in Early Modern Britain and Ireland* (New York: Oxford University Press, 2011).

Weinstock, Jeffrey Andrew, *Gothic Things: Dark Enchantment and Anthropocene Anxiety* (New York: Fordham University Press, 2023).

Wood, Robin, *Hollywood from Vietnam to Reagan* (New York: Columbia University Press, 1986).

Woodlands Dark and Days Bewitched: A History of Folk Horror, directed by Kier-La Janisse (Severin Films, 2021).

Cambridge Elements ☰

The Gothic

Dale Townshend
Manchester Metropolitan University
Dale Townshend is Professor of Gothic Literature in the Manchester Centre for Gothic Studies, Manchester Metropolitan University.

Angela Wright
University of Sheffield
Angela Wright is Professor of Romantic Literature in the School of English at the University of Sheffield and co-director of its Centre for the History of the Gothic.

About the Series
Seeking to publish short, research-led yet accessible studies of the foundational 'elements' within Gothic Studies as well as showcasing new and emergent lines of scholarly enquiry, this innovative series brings to a range of specialist and non-specialist readers some of the most exciting developments in recent Gothic scholarship.

Cambridge Elements ☰

The Gothic

Printed in the United States
by Baker & Taylor Publisher Services